# HOME IN

Welcome
Home!

Christa

# Hay House Titles of Related Interest

*YOU CAN HEAL YOUR LIFE,*
*the movie,* starring Louise Hay & Friends
(available as a 1-DVD program and an expanded 2-DVD set)
Watch the trailer at: www.LouiseHayMovie.com

*THE SHIFT, the movie,*
starring Dr. Wayne W. Dyer
(available as a 1-DVD program and an expanded 2-DVD set)
Watch the trailer at: www.DyerMovie.com

*THE EARTH DIET: Your Complete Guide to Living Using*
*Earth's Natural Ingredients,* by Liana Werner-Gray

*FENG SHUI FOR THE SOUL: How to Create a Harmonious*
*Environment That Will Nurture and Sustain You,*
by Denise Linn

*GREEN MADE EASY: The Everyday Guide for*
*Transitioning to a Green Lifestyle,* by Chris Prelitz

*MANIFEST MOMENT TO MOMENT: 8 Principles to Create*
*the Life Your Truly Desire,* by Tejpal and Dr. Carrol McLaughlin

*MINDFUL INTENTIONS,* by Louie Schwartzberg and Miraval

*SECRETS OF MEDITATION: A Practical Guide to*
*Inner Peace and Personal Transformation,* by davidji

All of the above are available at your local bookstore,
or may be ordered by visiting:

Hay House USA: www.hayhouse.com®
Hay House Australia: www.hayhouse.com.au
Hay House UK: www.hayhouse.co.uk
Hay House South Africa: www.hayhouse.co.za
Hay House India: www.hayhouse.co.in

# HOME IN
## *Harmony*
### DESIGNING AN INSPIRED LIFE

# CHRISTA O'LEARY

**HAY HOUSE, INC.**
Carlsbad, California • New York City
London • Sydney • Johannesburg
Vancouver • Hong Kong • New Delhi

*Published and distributed in the United States by:* Hay House, Inc.: www.hayhouse.com® • *Published and distributed in Australia by:* Hay House Australia Pty. Ltd.: www.hayhouse.com.au • *Published and distributed in the United Kingdom by:* Hay House UK, Ltd.: www.hayhouse.co.uk • *Published and distributed in the Republic of South Africa by:* Hay House SA (Pty), Ltd.: www.hayhouse.co.za • *Distributed in Canada by:* Raincoast Books: www.raincoast.com • *Published in India by:* Hay House Publishers India: www.hayhouse.co.in

*Cover design:* Stonesong • *Interior design:* Pamela Homan

### Library of Congress Cataloging-in-Publication Data

O'Leary, Christa, date.
 Home in harmony : designing an inspired life / Christa O'Leary.
 pages cm
 ISBN 978-1-4019-4328-8 (paperback)
1. Self-actualization (Psychology) 2. Motivation (Psychology)
3. Lifestyles. I. Title.
BF637.S4O4296 2014
158.1--dc23

                    2014011692


Tradepaper ISBN: 978-1-4019-4328-8

10  9  8  7  6  5  4  3  2  1
1st edition, November 2014

Printed in the United States of America

SUSTAINABLE FORESTRY INITIATIVE
Certified Chain of Custody
Promoting Sustainable Forestry
www.sfiprogram.org
SFI-01268
SFI label applies to the text stock

*In 1995, I was blessed to begin a journey with a partner who not only believed in me but who also accepted my complex fascination with life—to explore and understand every facet of it. Every cell in my being feels immense gratitude and love for my husband, Leif, who had a warm dinner waiting for me when I came home late from graduate school, encouraged me to take weekends away to fill my soul, and consistently tells me I can do anything I set my mind to. He radiates a positive, no-limits attitude that is contagious and has shown me that all things are possible when someone believes in you and helps you believe in yourself. I am blessed to share the adventures of parenthood with this man, whose strength and integrity are a beacon that guides our family. Thank you for your love, support, and wisdom every day. Thank you for always encouraging me to pursue my dreams. You are my rock, and I dedicate this book to you.*

*This book is also dedicated to four beautiful beings of light I am so thankful to have the privilege to guide and nurture. Bailey, Kiley, Clare, and Brenna, every day you teach me and challenge me to be the best I can be. My heart has felt such expansive joy and love with each new addition to Team O'Leary. Thank you for supporting me during this project! I love you guys and am happy to be your mom.*

# Contents

# A Note from the Author

Most people who meet me or get to know me would be surprised to learn that I was not always calm, happy, and organized. It took years for me to discover a deep inner peace and a profound sense of joy. I look back at my life and realize that my winding journey of good and bad experiences has created the person I am today, which makes me thankful for each sacred moment. These experiences have given me the foundation to teach a way of life that can bring joy, optimal health, and harmony.

I was trained from an early age to look good—literally—no matter how much turmoil was going on inside. Appearances were important, and a sunny disposition was expected regardless of the circumstances. It would take me years to actually feel the fun, enthusiasm, and joy that I had always projected to the world. For most of my life, I felt a sense of dread every morning. I didn't want to leave the safety of my bed. As I explored the worlds of psychology, yoga, spirituality, and healthy living, the wall I had built around myself, for what I

thought was self-preservation, began to crack. The sun started to shine through the cracks and melt away the fear and dread that had been unconsciously holding me back from living a harmonious and joyful life. With each new thing I learned, my self-imposed fortress crumbled more, and the sun grew brighter, warmer, and stronger. My spirit was set free! I realized the importance of sharing my insights with the world.

You should awaken to each new dawn with anticipation, truly knowing that your day has the potential to be filled with excitement, harmony, and unbridled joy. Let me share with you the elements of the Home in Harmony *Lifestyle,* how it changed my life, and how it can help you. I purposefully say *lifestyle* because this is a way of living. Embracing the concepts of Home in Harmony and weaving them into your daily routine will enable you to start enjoying the benefits. My story illustrates how *you* can begin designing *your* inspired life, your Home in Harmony Lifestyle.

I had a deep yearning from a very early age to understand why some people were happy and others were not. I was the observer, always watching and wondering. I noticed that money and privilege did not necessarily bring people happiness. As I looked around me in my upper-middle-class suburb, I witnessed most of my friends' parents go through divorce (along with mine). I saw many individuals who were lost in a fog of drugs or dependent on alcohol to get through their lives. My curiosity and deep longing to make sense of the world led me to the study of human development at Boston College, where I learned the core tenets of Western psychology. I still had questions, so I embarked on the study of marriage and family therapy in graduate school. Working with clients and groups gave me a deeper understanding of the "dance" between people—and how some interactions flowed gracefully but many others did not.

I gave up practicing marriage and family therapy following the birth of my first child, Bailey, in 1997. After 14 hours of labor, the doctors realized I had a life-threatening complication called HELLP syndrome. With this condition, your blood doesn't coagulate and your vital organs begin shutting down, starting with your liver. I was raced into the operating room for an emergency C-section. The OR was a fusion of bright lights; people moving briskly; clanging surgical equipment; and jolts of excruciating pain from my contractions, one on top of the other like waves in the ocean. This unpleasant environment suddenly went dim and transformed into a serene space filled with a loving light that warmed my being. I felt bliss, gratitude, and all-consuming love. This was the ultimate Savasana—that is, an extreme version of the peace engendered by that yoga pose. I loved this place, and I never wanted to leave. I longed for more. Then a loving but firm voice said, "It is not your time. You have work to do." The soft light and serenity began to fade away, drowned out by a buzz of chaos, harsh light, and agonizing pain that ripped through my body.

I was in the intensive care unit for ten days and was not supposed to have any visitors. I was in such a weak state that I wasn't even supposed to see the baby. I remotely remembered from a Lamaze class I took that the mother had the right to make whatever requests she wanted regarding the birth and the baby. Despite the doctor's objections, I insisted on having the baby stay

in my room. I think his presence helped me regain my strength and my will to live. Needless to say, my near-death experience (NDE) had a huge impact on my view of the world and our experience as infinite beings in it.

For the next five years, I focused on my fabulous husband and our decision to bring three more beautiful beings of light into the world. I created a home environment that was emotionally and aesthetically nurturing. Everyone who came into our home would comment on how peaceful it was or how beautiful it looked. Friends and acquaintances would tease me that I was like Martha Stewart because my house was attractive and organized, I came up with creative ideas for decorating and entertaining, and I was a do-it-yourself type of person. I began to help people decorate their homes and come up with fun party ideas.

During that time, we realized Bailey had an anaphylactic allergy to milk protein. At nine months old, he turned blue at his first drop of milk. So we began the arduous process of learning about *all* the foods we brought into our home. I would spend hours at the grocery store examining the ingredients listed on packages. If I didn't know what some ten-letter substance was, I would write it down and spend hours more researching it . . . Google didn't exist yet.

This process was not only challenging but also eye-opening! By deciphering labels, I deepened my awareness of what was in our food. I had always been self-taught regarding nutrition. (The graduate student in me loves learning and researching until I find answers that make sense.) At one point, after years of struggling with yo-yo dieting, stomachaches, skin rashes, and lackluster health, I became interested in finding a better way. The ultimate catalyst was a severe systemic yeast infection (different from a superficial yeast infection, such as oral thrush or vaginitis), which caused me to have an all-over body rash and began to affect my breathing. Western doctors would prescribe pills that initially managed the situation but then created a boomerang effect that left me feeling sicker than before. When I finally went the holistic route, I began to develop an awareness of how I felt after eating different foods. My investigations and observations helped me uncover the toxins in our food, and I have since adopted a clean-eating lifestyle.

My natural curiosity led me to investigate feng shui, the "Chinese philosophical system of harmonizing the human existence with the surrounding environment."[1] Feng shui was a perfect blend of the things I loved: home and psychology. The practice of feng shui made sense to me as a Western-educated psychology grad. I saw the connection between the principles of feng shui and psychology. For example, according to feng shui, bed position can have a huge impact on a person's life. From a psychological perspective, it made sense to me that one's bed should face the door. Another position would unconsciously evoke the brain's fight-or-flight response, which would then not allow you to get a good night's sleep—affecting your performance and mood the next day.

At the time I began to explore feng shui, yoga became a bigger part of my life. I met teachers who would expand my horizons by introducing me to meditation, affirmation work, and mindfulness. My curiosity about the metaphysical world grew and grew, and I became a student not only of feng shui but also of dowsing, space clearing, and reiki. My studies led me to two amazing

feng shui teachers who were also interior designers and certified green designers. (Green design is environmentally conscious design that is committed to sustainability.) I studied under these highly regarded mentors for a number of years. As I learned more about green design, I began to realize that many of the products that were unhealthy to have in our homes were the same ones I had found on food labels years earlier. Chemicals that were too toxic to breathe were *in our food!* So began my mission to teach the average mom what she was bringing home to her family, from furniture to mattresses to rugs to drinking water to food.

In 2006, my interior design career really began to take off when I was chosen to participate in two consecutive show houses. (A show house showcases the work of various designers, who compete for space within a home that is going to be totally redone and then opened for the public to see. Prospective designers must put together a concept board, which goes in front of a panel of judges.) My work was published in the Home sections of national newspapers across the country and was featured on NBC. Various publications called to ask if I had rooms designed in specific ways that they could spotlight. The pinnacle of this experience occurred when a major international fabric house, Kravet Fabrics, featured one of my rooms on its website between articles about Calvin Klein and Candice Olson.

What amazed most people was that I was able to create a booming business, have fun with friends, volunteer for the PTO (parent teacher organization), maintain my wellness regime of working out and practicing yoga, and raise a beautiful family—all while keeping a sense of calm, harmony, peace, and love.

The summer after my debut as a rising star in the interior design world, my husband's job changed, and we needed to move to a different state. I had built a business based on a collaborative model, working with specialty painters, upholstery workrooms, and a host of other vendors within my industry. I would have to leave all of them behind and virtually give up my business.

The move compelled me to evaluate what made it possible for me to live a vibrant, energized, and fulfilled life. Because we were starting over, I had to build a *new* life for myself and my family. And I was successful. People who know me, have briefly met me, or have heard my story continuously come up to me asking how I manage everything I do . . . especially because all four of my kids play hockey! My own journey has allowed me to create a joyful and fulfilling lifestyle, one that is easy to maintain and simple to teach.

When I step back and look at my life, I see a rich, luxurious tapestry woven from a vibrant array of colorful threads. At this distance, a beautiful pattern emerges. But my individual life experiences—the separate strands within the tapestry—didn't make sense at first, because they were so varied. Similarly, the individual components of the Home in Harmony Lifestyle, which are called "pillars," have significance on their own—but together they create a truly inspired life.

I hope you will use the simple solutions offered by the Home in Harmony Lifestyle to help you design the magnificent tapestry of your life.

Many blessings,
**Christa**

# Introduction to the Home in Harmony Lifestyle

Imagine waking up in the morning revived, refreshed, and exuberant to face the day. As your eyes begin to focus, you look around your bedroom with sheer gratitude at the serene space you have created. It has fortified you with a good night's sleep. You think of the many things for which you are grateful, setting the tone for the day. Jotting down these thoughts of appreciation acknowledges the grace in your life, which opens you to notice and receive even greater abundance. You take a few moments to visualize a day of ease and joy. Before your feet even touch the floor, you drink a few glasses of water. You know this practice will help wake up your body, flush out toxins, and diminish a false sense of hunger. Hydrating your body also leads to radiant skin. As you finish your ten-minute routine of gracefully getting out of bed, you feel inspired to greet the day, your kids, and your coworkers. You feel vibrantly alive, grounded, and clear.

Next, you engage in a routine of movement. Getting the blood pumping, sweating out toxins, losing weight, and stimulating "happy" hormones all contribute to a sense of joy that has a huge beneficial impact on your overall well-being. Paradoxically, this physical activity helps connect you to a deep stillness within. You move efficiently through your well-organized kitchen, filled with healthful, nutrient-dense superfoods that allow your body to run optimally and reduce your family's chance of serious illness. As steam fills the shower, you take a deep breath, knowing that the water is free of toxins, the cleansers used to clean your bathroom are healthful and won't release toxic off-gasses, and the shampoo and soap you are putting on your body are chemical-free. As you grab your towel and pat droplets of water from your face, you are cognizant that your linens are *not* coated with the synthetic chemicals found in most laundry detergents.

Easily and without much thought, you grab your keys, which are always located in the same spot—eliminating the frustration that comes from not being able to find the things needed in your daily routine. As you glance around, it is evident that your home environment supports you and your family. It is aesthetically pleasing; you love the colors and the artwork. You look forward to returning later in the day, when you will curl up on your cozy couch with a cup of tea and a good book.

Your day includes an array of appointments, commitments, and communications. You notice friends or colleagues heading to the vending machine or coffee shop for a pick-me-up. You also observe that you *don't* have cravings for sugar or caffeine, which, in the past, would have given you a burst of energy and then left you crashing. Your energy remains vigorous and clear. If, at any point, you notice fogginess in your mind, you take a few minutes to breathe deeply and reconnect to the vibrancy within. Speaking of vibrancy, you glow! Your eyes sparkle with joy and vitality. Your radiance, which results from your inspired life, naturally and graciously magnetizes positive people and situations to you. Others want to be around you, new blessings show up, and experiences of abundance unfold.

Does all of this sound attainable? It is—and more! This is the Home in Harmony Lifestyle. This is the life I lead every day and the lifestyle I have taught to people who, in turn, have created their own magnificently inspired lives. The following pages will provide a clear guide for creating your inspired life. You will begin to notice which aspects of your current life are habitually toxic and destructive. Awakening your innate power of conscious decision making is the first step in designing your most fulfilled life.

The four "pillars," or foundational elements, of the Home in Harmony Lifestyle are an inspired home, a healthy body, a calm mind, and inner light. Let's take a quick look at these pillars.

1. *An inspired home.* Your home environment either nurtures you or drains your energy. You either walk into your house and say, "Thank goodness I'm home," or you see distressing clutter and things that need to be fixed.

2. *A healthy body.* There is an old saying that if you don't have your health, you don't have anything. Your physical health affects every

other area of your life. It is important to create a body full of energy and vitality.

3. *A calm mind.* It is vital to find calm in the midst of our chaotic world, which seems to be moving faster and faster. Achieving a tranquil, clear mind is critical to leading your best life.

4. *Inner light.* Studies have shown that a critical component of attaining bliss is finding your life's purpose and sharing it with the world.

My hope is that as you read this book and examine the current patterns of your life, you will begin to develop an awareness of negative habits. The Home in Harmony Lifestyle lets you replace these life-draining thoughts and actions with uplifting and life-giving routines. The book's organization supports this goal. In the first chapter, we will examine the role of habits in your daily activities. Becoming aware of your habits is the first step in changing your life, because it gives you the power to make *different* choices. The next four chapters address, in turn, the four pillars of the Home in Harmony Lifestyle. I will guide you toward creating an inspired home, attaining a healthy body, achieving a calm mind, and sharing your inner light joyously with the world. In the final chapter, I will help you use the blueprint of the Home in Harmony Lifestyle to take action in building your own extraordinary life. Throughout, I will provide insights, examples, and tips to awaken you to your true potential. In addition, each chapter features simple "Harmony in Action" exercises that allow you to ponder and practice the ideas presented. Be sure to refer to the two appendices at the back of the book; they are treasure troves of information that will support you, very practically, as you begin to implement the Home in Harmony Lifestyle.

As you go through these pages, keep the following questions in mind:

- What can you do to begin designing a home that fortifies your soul?

- What healthy eating habits can you implement in your life?

- How will you move from chaos to calm?

- What fills your spirit and helps you shine your light?

By the time you finish reading *Home in Harmony*, you will be able to answer these questions and many others regarding the four pillars that structurally support an inspired life. This knowledge will allow you to take steps toward leading an existence filled with joy, peace, and abundance. So let's get started!

*Chapter One*

# The Role of Habits in Your Life

An overriding requirement for finding harmony, peace, good health, and vitality is an awareness of habits. These repetitive thoughts and actions take place on a daily basis and determine whether you move through life with ease and grace or with agitation and discontent. As you read this chapter, begin to notice which of your thoughts and actions are motivated by ingrained and unconscious routines. Be open to observing where habits show up for you. These behaviors might have taken a lifetime to develop or are suggested by the noisy world around us. Identifying negative habits creates a momentum of awareness that can facilitate great change. Your new perspective will allow you to make positive and life-affirming choices for your home, body, mind, and spirit.

First, let's look at the concept of habits, how and why habits form, and in what ways they truly affect you.

## *The Habits of a Typical Lifestyle*

It is hard to fathom that the majority of our thoughts, words, and actions are generated without conscious awareness. Yes, you read that correctly. Much of our daily activity is habitual. We walk around in a daze, unwittingly relinquishing the power to make conscious decisions. Some habits are positive, like grabbing your towel before you get into the shower each morning. Other habits, like running to the kitchen for an extra cookie because you are feeling stressed, can have a detrimental effect on your overall well-being. The key is to unlock the chains of limiting and destructive habits so you can live fully and freely in the present, able to make conscious, clear, and life-affirming choices. Taking the veil off your habits is like seeing the clear blue sky on a sunny spring day. Let's look at why the veil is there and how to remove it now and forever.

## Behavioral Habits

A few months ago, I purchased a beautiful silver container to hold cotton swabs in my bathroom. It was just what I was looking for! Decorative and pretty, it gave me the sense of elegant luxury to which I am drawn. On a practical level, it would help my morning routine flow with ease and grace. The cotton swabs would be within arm's reach; I wouldn't have to bend down to grab them from lower in the bathroom vanity. This was helpful because I had dislodged one of the disks in my back while doing a yoga move on a paddleboard a few months earlier, and bending down was painful. I thought my purchase was clever because, aesthetically, it made me smile, *and* it served a useful purpose. However, I didn't use it! Why? Because my habitual behavior was so ingrained that I unconsciously bent down to grab the cotton swabs before I could even think about it. Thankfully, I was able to laugh at myself and see the genius of the universe's gift of insight—which we all can see if we are awake enough to use it. This was the perfect illustration of a habit to share with you!

It was amazing to me that although I could clearly see my chronic pattern, I still had trouble changing it—even with the beautiful container in view! I realized that not only did I have to make the desired behavior easy to achieve, I had to create an obstacle for the undesired action: I removed the cotton swabs from the cabinet. Consciously manipulating patterns in this way can be helpful. Removing the thing we wish to stop and replacing it with something positive can often interrupt the habitual cycle. Later in this chapter, I will explain how to do this.

At a few points in my life, I was hooked on items I consumed. The first was diet soda, when I was in college. Initially, I didn't realize I had an issue—who ever says they are addicted to soda? And back in the early 90s, unlike today, consumers didn't know how unhealthy soda was for the body. I was drinking a great deal of soda and continuously having stomachaches—but I didn't connect the two. One day, my observant roommate asked me if I knew how many diet soft drinks I consumed a day. I truly had no idea. I decided to set up an experiment. On a random, ordinary day, I tracked the number of diet sodas I drank. By the end of the day, I realized I had consumed 13! I was shocked. I had

no idea I was drinking a case of soda every two days. I was thankful that my roommate had brought this unconscious behavior to my awareness—the first step in habit modification.

By becoming aware of a pattern, we are able to change it. When I recognized that I was drinking an excessive amount of soda, I was in a position to determine if I wanted to keep this behavior or change it. Intuitively, I knew that my stomachaches were due in part—if not entirely—to this overconsumption. I also knew that to change my habit, I needed to choose a healthy replacement and remove the temptation of diet soda from my routine. I understood that the substitute had to be as convenient as diet soda; otherwise, I would fail. Initially, to quench my cravings, I swapped diet soda for water, seltzer water, and juice. I also took different routes on campus, to avoid going past soda machines at several points in my day. These efforts helped me change my habitual behavior—which helped my body move back into balance. My painful stomachaches, which had taken a toll on my overall sense of well-being, stopped.

## Mental Habits

Habits are not limited to physical actions but are found in our thoughts, as well. Thoughts are powerful tools that can help us or hurt us. Positive thought patterns are advantageous to our overall well-being. Negative thought patterns, however, can have the opposite effect. Messages you learned early in life (such as that you can't accomplish something because you aren't good at it) can become so ingrained in your belief system that you accept and act (or don't act) on them, even if they are completely untrue. Despite the fact that you are older, wiser, and stronger now, the negative beliefs you acquired as a child can hold you back; they can sabotage you. The key is to understand what habits are and where they have formed in your life.

## What Are Habits?

It is important to look at why we form habits because, in and of themselves, they are not necessarily bad. On the contrary, habits can be positive and life-affirming. First, it is important to understand what a habit is. *Merriam-Webster Dictionary* defines habit as "an acquired mode of behavior that has become nearly or completely involuntary" and "a behavior pattern acquired by frequent repetition or physiologic exposure that shows itself in regularity or increased facility of performance."[1] In other words, a habit is a way of acting that becomes almost automatic because you do it repeatedly.

It is fascinating to think of all the areas in our lives that rely on completely involuntary actions. Consider, for example, your morning routine. Do you really think about each step? Your brain can function on autopilot because you have repeated the same performance so many times before. Therefore, you are free to think about other things, such as the day ahead. This natural ability to act unconsciously is effective when the behaviors involved are positive or don't need attention from a safety standpoint. But if the behaviors are negative or dangerous, to do them unconsciously could be detrimental. Think about the times you have driven a

distance and can't remember doing so because you had "zoned out." Your brain was on autopilot. Other potentially harmful habits include smoking, overeating, procrastinating, worrying, watching too much television, gossiping, overspending, lying, and not getting enough sleep, just to name a few. Begin to be mindful of your everyday activities and notice how often autopilot overrides your conscious awareness.

Habits form by repeating a behavior over and over. Eventually, we shift from thinking about the activity to being on autopilot because the sequence involving the behavior has embedded itself in the neural synaptic pathways (the impulse part) of the brain. Science is at odds as to how long it takes for the pattern to become ingrained, but typically a habit needs as little as three weeks to form. Scientists do agree that a habit is triggered by a cue that sets the behavioral routine in motion. Doing the behavior produces a reward (some sort of gratification), which compels you to repeat the behavior the next time the cue occurs. With repetition, the behavior becomes fortified in the brain—creating a habit.

Some scientists feel that habits can be entirely replaced, while others argue that habits can be *substituted for* but will always lie dormant within the brain's pathways.[2] The latter claim explains why after years of abstinence from smoking, drinking, or taking drugs, recovered substance users can relapse when something triggers the response mechanism in the brain. Keep in mind that habits have three components: (1) the trigger or cue that leads to (2) the activity or process that becomes embedded because of (3) the anticipation of a reward. Recognizing that this pattern may, in fact, lie dormant unless and until it is triggered (even if you have replaced it with a new habit) is fundamental to becoming fully awake. If you have this awareness, when a trigger is present, you can consciously disempower it. In this way, you can free yourself from the constraints of old patterns.

During graduate school, I studied for countless hours, had a practical internship seeing clients with mental health issues, bartended and waitressed to pay the rent, and had fun with friends. During this period, there was so much to fit into each day. Therefore, my days would start early, and my nights would sometimes turn into day as I was cramming for tests and finishing up projects. To make it through, I developed a habit of drinking an inordinate amount of coffee. Initially, I would have an extra-large French vanilla Dunkin' Donuts coffee with two sugars and skim milk. As my caffeine tolerance grew and my energy level decreased, I added a daily coffee stop. Eventually, I was drinking *three* extra-large coffees to make it through the day. I didn't have the awareness to step back and look at what was truly going on. I was on autopilot, unconscious of the fact that my body and my life were out of balance.

Unless we begin to examine our lives, we can remain unaware of our negative habits—until something jolts us awake. My body began to communicate to me that my lifestyle choices were taking a toll. Sharp abdominal pains would wake me up at night and sometimes leave me bent over while waitressing. I found out that I had developed an ulcer. The doctor explained that coffee was literally eating away at my insides, and I needed to change my intake. I realized that I was pushing myself physically and emotionally every day. My exhaustion had triggered the action of drinking coffee. The reward

of drinking coffee was that I felt revived, at least initially. As the caffeine high from one coffee became less effective, I began to introduce more. Each additional beverage reinforced the habitual sequence in my brain—which threw my natural rhythm increasingly out of balance.

The ulcer was a wake-up call from my body. I evaluated how I could modify my daily routine to feel less exhausted. Making changes helped me have more energy, so I didn't have to rely on caffeine. I then replaced coffee with healthier options, such as green tea and lemon water. Even after all this time, the delicious aroma of coffee triggers an emotional and physical response for me. But conscious awareness gives me clarity when exhaustion sets in and allows me to make supportive and healthy choices.

## How Do Habits Serve Us?

Understanding how habits *serve* us is important. It is okay to do things unconsciously if they are good for us! Habits can help us live vibrant, healthy, and joyful lives. First, we must begin the process of removing the veil—the unconscious aspect—of habit formation, which can be detrimental and constricting. As *Merriam-Webster Dictionary* also states, habit is a "characteristic mode of growth."[3] Nature has designed patterns of growth that are characteristic of a species to promote its development and maturation. Some of these patterns are instincts, which are designed to aid the advancement of the individual and the species. For survival, birds fly south in the winter, bears hibernate, and jellyfish follow currents of warm water. Polar bears are born with an insatiable appetite. This internal mechanism allows them to store fat for long periods—which can help them survive when they are unable to find food for months at a time. This balancing system contributes to the order of the natural world.

Autopilot patterns serve birds, bears, and jellyfish, and they can serve us, too. While instincts are inborn and habits are learned, there is a connection between the two. The brain is on autopilot for both. In this mode, behavior is controlled by an internal process that is beyond conscious awareness. I will give you a personal example of running on autopilot. With my kids in high school, middle school, and elementary school, our morning program has several shifts. First, I make my son, who is in high school, an omelet and multiple sandwiches for his lunch. He has to be driven to the pickup location two hours before the littlest one needs to be walked to the bus. Between these activities, four breakfasts have to be made, lunches prepared, and middle schoolers ushered out the door. As the youngest is getting ready to leave, we are multitasking—tying ponytails, matching socks, and signing paperwork for school. Thankfully, my brain automatically knows that I want to put my sneakers on. My fingers take over and tie the laces without any thought on my part. This is useful if I am helping the little one match mittens and gloves; in other words, I can focus mentally on another task while I am tying my shoes.

Putting on my sneakers initiates a positive habitual routine for me. After kissing my youngest goodbye and watching her climb the steps of the bus, I begin my morning run. At that point, I am outside, running shoes on and ready to go. I have created a positive habit that

allows me to sidestep contemplating whether or not I am going to get out and exercise. If I were to stop and think about running, there is a chance I would distract myself with one of a hundred other tasks, never making it out the door with my running shoes on. Two rewards occur after my run: Gratifying endorphins kick in, and I gift myself with a few moments of centering meditation. Both of these benefits make me want to come back for more exercise, day after day. The exercise component of my morning routine produces vitality, good health, and a sense of well-being. Like this, many habits can serve you.

Habits are *not* beneficial when they create a disturbance in your emotional or physical system. If birds flew north in winter, they would be hard-pressed to survive, for lack of food. In a similar way, if you or I were to adopt habits that threw us out of balance, our well-being would suffer. Therefore, it is important to reflect on the habits that exist in your life. Begin to remove the veil of unconsciousness from your experience to gain a clearer picture of how you move through your day. You *can* become fully conscious, purposefully choosing your thoughts, words, and actions.

## Shifting Habitual Programming

Beginning to modify the habits that are keeping you from having an inspired life requires you to do three things:

1. Become consciously aware of your habits
2. Understand the dynamics that drive habits
3. Recognize how your habits are serving you

The first step in becoming a conscious creator of your life experience is to notice which behaviors you do in autopilot mode. Evaluate whether these unconscious behaviors are life-giving or life-draining. For each one, ask yourself, "Do I want this in my life?" Stepping out of autopilot mode is easiest when you look at your daily routine and ask yourself why you do certain things. It can also help to ask trusted, supportive individuals in your life if they have noticed any patterns. Recognizing these patterns gives you your power back by allowing you to make conscious choices.

Understanding how habits work is the second step in shifting your unconscious behaviors. Realizing that habits consist of a three-part sequence (trigger, activity, and reward) helps you recognize what prompts you to do things—and to keep doing them. Identifying the needs you are hoping to fulfill and why they exist gives you clarity about your behavior.

In today's culture, it is typical for people to want instant gratification. But instead of seeking immediate satisfaction, take time to examine the root of your needs. Step back and really determine if a pattern is in your best interest and highest good. Ask yourself, "Is this behavior serving me?" When you begin to see areas in your life that are not working optimally, you can start the process of making changes—replacing negative habits with supportive ones.

## Unconscious Seeds of Habit

It is now more important than ever to evaluate our habitual patterns. In today's world, we are inundated

with influences vying for our attention and intentionally trying to create habits in our lives. Becoming aware of our own habits and how habits form minimizes the influence of others' opinions and suggestions in our lives. We move from a place of veiled, or ambiguous, perception, where outside influences try to plant the seeds of habit, to a place of clarity about the intentions of society and business. This shift restores your personal power and your ability to determine which habits you choose to welcome into your life.

## The Marketing Machine

It is truly eye-opening to step back and view the cultural influences on our habitual behaviors. Even more astonishing is to recognize how the goal of industry is to *start habits in our lives*. When businesses have achieved their seeding in your neural pathways, you can potentially become a customer for life. Understanding the nuts and bolts of advertising is critical in our society, because we are inundated by advertisements every day—through radio, magazines, newspapers, billboards, television, and the Internet. Advertising is a multibillion-dollar industry. If it didn't have a powerful effect on our buying behavior, businesses wouldn't spend so much money on it. As a culture, we allow advertisers more direct access to us than ever before, because we are constantly tuned in to media. Through this nonstop connection, marketers influence the things we bring into our homes, ingest, or apply to our bodies—shaping our thinking and decision making. Gaining this awareness is the first step in decreasing the power that advertising holds over us.

As the daughter of an advertising and marketing businessperson, I was exposed from a young age to the strategies companies use to promote products. I would often hear about the campaigns involved in marketing plans. I found these discussions so intriguing. They often revolved around finding something people needed or couldn't live without, or creating a dilemma that only this product—which might be a person, place, thing, or state of mind—could resolve. It was as if the marketers were actually trying to *create* the problem! As a child, I didn't fully understand this rationale, because I could see through the deception. Now I not only see through the deception but understand that companies manipulate consumers in this way because it increases profits. Thus, the objective of business is to find or create a problem and then supply its solution, for immediate relief or gratification. When advertisers are in the initial stages of designing a campaign, they try to identify the need that will trigger the purchase of whatever they are selling. The more they can convince you that their product will solve your woes, the more likely you are to buy it. If they can keep convincing you that the product satisfies your ongoing dilemma, the more likely your buying decision will develop into a buying habit.

My son was early to say his first word, and by the time he was a little over two, he would chat away nonstop. As we drove around town, from his car seat, he would joyfully point at everything he saw and announce its name: "Truck!" "Car!" "Tree!" His big blue eyes would sparkle with delight when he connected an object with what it was called. Soon, he was able to add descriptions, calling objects "brown bird" or "blue car," for example. It was fun to listen to the excitement in his voice as he

articulated the world around him. One day, as we were passing Starbucks, he pointed to the pretty green mermaid and exclaimed, "Venti decaf nonfat mocha Frappuccino!" I was aghast! That moment was another that woke me up from my unconscious behavior. It also demonstrated the influence of marketing and the power of habit formation. Bailey saw the sign, which triggered the response of ordering a drink. This connection had no doubt formed because when I ordered a Venti decaf nonfat mocha Frappuccino, he would sometimes get a treat.

To get an idea of how many buying habits have been created in your life, think about the last time you went to the grocery store. Did you ever notice that all the stores for a particular chain are set up exactly the same, from the configuration of the aisles to the placement of products within the aisles? This pattern encourages autopilot mode; you navigate by habit. You don't need to think about which bread to buy, for instance, because your subconscious knows just where it is; you can grab it and keep moving. The supermarkets and manufacturers desire this behavior because they don't want you to stop and think, even for a second. If you stop and think, you might decide to try something new—or choose not to purchase anything at all. It behooves them to make grocery shopping an easy experience, one in which you operate unconsciously.

The finesse of strategy marketing is also illustrated when you go into a store for one thing and come out with additional items that you may not have needed. I often hear of people shopping at one of the large, membership-only warehouse stores and returning home with all sorts of things they didn't require or necessarily desire—but the purchases seemed like good ideas at the time. These decisions are considered "impulse buying," and they result from a great sales strategy. Retail establishments use a variety of psychological principles and techniques to lure potential customers through the door and then keep them there. The longer customers are in a store, the more likely they are to buy.

One tactic is the utilization of scent. Studies have shown that using the aroma of vanilla in a retail store increases the amount of time and money women are likely to spend there.[4] A Rutgers University study also found a positive correlation between "pleasant background music" and "unplanned purchases."[5] Being alert to the psychological devices used to steer your actions gives you more clarity in your decision making. The next time you walk into a store and think, "Ah, that smells good," remember that scent is a marketing strategy to get you to stay and buy something.

Again, our behavior reflects the power of marketing. Take a look around your home to see the evidence. Examine why you chose certain items. Were you truly inspired, or did you think having a particular item would make you feel better in some way? Maybe, along the way, someone told you it was the product for you, and your life would benefit from it.

Have you ever bought that "special something," only to find that it lost its "shine" a few weeks later? The purchase gave you instant gratification, but you began to feel less satisfied with it even as you left the store. Because you move through your day largely unconsciously, the "marketing machine" is able to steer you in the direction of making specific purchases. Awareness of this artful attempt to influence your behavior moves you

from functioning on autopilot to being a laser-focused, informed decision maker.

Studies have shown that satisfaction with life in our highly technological Western culture is lower than in some less developed countries.[6] We are continuously striving to do, have, and be more. Essentially, we have been programmed to look outside ourselves for contentment. In recent years, it has become customary to reward young children simply for participating on athletic teams, regardless of whether they perform with excellence, dedication, or heart. No longer do children derive satisfaction from playing a sport they love, on a team with their buddies; rather, their focus is, "Will I get a trophy for this season, or this tournament?" We are shifting our children's attention from enjoying the activity to seeking a tangible reward. Therefore, they do not experience an internal sense of satisfaction; rather, joy and fulfillment come from the outside. This early model fosters the need for more and more concrete gratification, until a habit is formed. The coffee habit I mentioned earlier in this chapter was similar; I needed more and more of the stimulus.

To reiterate, begin to examine everything you purchase, determining which of your buying decisions are habits. Are these habits truly beneficial—or unnecessary and possibly detrimental? As a culture, we are bombarded by outside influences that distract us from our innate ability to identify things, people, and experiences that support us. By reflecting on your buying behavior and analyzing advertising campaigns, you can consciously choose the products you bring into your home.

## The Whirlwind Western Lifestyle

The fast pace of the Western lifestyle also increases the likelihood of habitual pattern formation. As a culture, we are moving at a rate that would have defied comprehension 25 years ago. Many of us are caught up in the rat race, striving to survive. We take on multiple tasks and activities, forcing our brain to revert to autopilot mode so we can accomplish several things at once. Becoming aware of when you multitask, and what activities you perform on autopilot, increases your awareness of your habitual patterns. You can then determine which activities you are able to execute effectively and efficiently in autopilot mode and which ones deserve or require your conscious attention. Actively choosing which autopilot patterns to keep will help you navigate today's complex world.

The Western lifestyle can make you feel like a driver strapped into a speeding racecar. Maneuvering turns, avoiding obstacles, ignoring distractions, and ultimately reaching the finish line all require targeted actions on your part. You may be able to accomplish some of these actions in autopilot mode, but others demand thoughtful decision making. It is critical to distinguish between the two, so you can make conscious choices when it is beneficial to do so.

## Harmony in Action

For the next seven days, do the following:

1.  Notice three things you do, say, or think in autopilot mode.

2.   Notice which pieces of advertising entice you.

3.   Notice which stores you are excited to shop in and why.

Most people walk around in a daze, allowing auto-pilot to take over and bring *them* along for the ride. This approach doesn't allow you to experience life on *your* terms. It puts you on a haphazard path, subject to the influence of outside forces. Becoming swept up in the momentum of external stimuli, such as marketing, sup-presses your conscious decision making and denies you the amazing gift of co-creation. From now on, as you move through your day, start to become aware of the thoughts, words, and actions that are on replay. Practic-ing mindfulness around your habits puts you in a posi-tion to modify them in order to help you design your inspired life. This idea is the cornerstone of the Home in Harmony Lifestyle, and we will apply it first to how you function in your living environment.

*Chapter Two*

# The First Pillar:
# An Inspired Home

An inspired home is the first pillar of the Home in Harmony Lifestyle. Your home environment either nurtures you or drains your energy. To put it another way, every time you walk into your house, you are either uplifted or depleted. This response can be felt on a physical, mental, or spiritual level. Creating a space that elevates and supports you is the first step in designing your best life.

This chapter provides guidelines for creating a home that is aesthetically attractive, environmentally healthful, and spiritually nourishing. You will gain a clear understanding of the products, materials, and design of the average Western home and how these factors influence your comfort, fulfillment, and health. The inspired

home pillar of the Home in Harmony Lifestyle offers you solutions for creating a living space that is nontoxic, beautiful, and sacred.

## Toxic Home

An impressive variety of products go into constructing, cleaning, and beautifying our homes. A few that come to mind are rugs, couches, bedding, cleaning products, and air fresheners. Understanding which of these products contain ingredients that are safe or hazardous is imperative to creating a healthy, nontoxic home. Approximately 80,000 chemicals make up the products that the average person brings home.[1] Only a small portion of these chemicals have been tested, and an even smaller portion are considered not harmful to humans. Additionally, the Environmental Protection Agency (EPA) has confirmed that the 1976 Toxic Substances Control Act allows chemical manufacturers to keep 20 percent of their ingredients secret.[2] Products considered benign for human exposure have been tested with a limited degree of usage, and not in combination with other chemicals that are used simultaneously. We are now learning that the combination and inundation of certain chemicals are creating a "toxic body burden" for the average person. This condition correlates to the frightening increase of dis-ease in our society. Because of their smaller body mass, children are impacted by chemicals even more greatly than adults. (We will talk more about toxic body burden in the next chapter.)

The question is, Do you really know what you are bringing into your home, even when you choose products that claim to be healthy and safe? Are these products truly healthy and safe for you, your family, and the Earth? Or are they part of a marketing ploy designed to create habitual buying patterns? Let's explore some of these items to see how they really stack up. This knowledge will empower you to choose which materials, products, and chemicals are appropriate to bring into your sanctuary.

## What Are You Bringing into Your Home?

Consider the following scenario, which may be familiar to you. At the grocery store, you pick up organic food items as well as other, more convenient family favorites; unscented laundry detergent and fabric softener in "green"-looking containers; and a few "green" cleaning supplies from one of the major brands. You feel great about your choices, thankful that you are more aware regarding products than people were in earlier generations. Returning home, you put the groceries away, start a load of laundry, pull on a cozy fleece sweatshirt made from recycled plastic bottles, and curl up on the couch to read and catch your breath for at least a moment. You are really starting to enjoy this room since thoughtfully choosing paint in the perfect color, from a major manufacturer boasting a product with low VOCs (volatile organic compounds, which are known carcinogens when inhaled).

Unfortunately, you have unwittingly been manipulated into buying and breathing in paint that *claims* minimal toxic off-gassing (emission of noxious gases) but is filled with VOCs by the time you get it home. (I

will share more on how this happens later.) Likewise, the comfortable sofa you are sitting on contains a host of toxic chemicals that you are unknowingly inhaling. These chemicals were listed as harmful and hazardous to production workers during the manufacturing process. But by the time the furniture found its way into the showroom and then into your home, the warnings had vanished.

The recycled sweatshirt you are wearing warms your body and feels soft against your skin. It also pleases your conscience: You have helped the Earth by purchasing a product that uses recycled plastic bottles, which otherwise would have ended up in a landfill. The unfortunate reality, however, is that to manipulate those bottles into a form never intended for plastic is a difficult process requiring more energy than creating a product from a non-recycled source. In a similar vein, you are thankful you have finally found a laundry detergent and fabric softener that work well and are healthy for you and the planet . . . at least that's what the labels suggest. However, often when a product is called "unscented," harmful chemicals have been added to eliminate the scent.

For your family's dinner, you have decided to make a salad of organic and conventionally grown vegetables, with marinated grilled chicken. As you begin to wash the produce under tap water, you are not aware of the multitude of pollutants you are exposing your food to. Unfiltered tap water may contain heavy metals as well as fluoride or chlorine purposely added to kill bacteria. By rinsing your vegetables in this cocktail, you are essentially putting chemicals into your body. The conventionally grown produce also contains a wide range of toxins that create havoc in the body. (I will discuss these toxins in the next chapter. My website, www.christaoleary.com, also lists food pesticides to avoid.) The grilled chicken seems like a healthy choice, but many of the leading brands give their chickens hormones and feed them pesticide-ridden or genetically modified grains—which end up in your body. As you step outside to grill the chicken, you breathe in the fresh early evening air—air that is actually filled with harmful industrial contaminants from around the globe. As you step back inside and close the sliding glass door, the air you breathe can be two to five times *more* toxic than the industrial pollution outside.[3]

You try to make the healthiest choices possible for yourself, your family, and the Earth. You have begun to see the impact of unhealthy products around you as cancer rates rise and the incidence of obesity and other dis-eases increases. You want better choices and safer options. You want to know what you are *really* buying and the true effects of these products on you and your family. But where do you go for the truth when companies often do not practice transparency and continue to offer products based on profit instead of the good of consumers? The following pages will begin to make sense of the puzzle, allowing you to prudently determine which goods and materials enter your home.

## Two Important Cycles

Two cycles illustrate how toxins affect us every day. First, the life cycle of toxins shows what these chemicals are and where they come from. Going a little deeper, the cycle of toxins in the body reveals what happens when

people ingest, inhale, or absorb these poisons. Knowing the nature and effects of toxins will hopefully prompt you to implement a clean lifestyle and devise ways to contend with these unavoidable noxious substances. The health of you and your family is at stake.

### The Life Cycle of Toxins

Following is a simple look at the complex processes involved in the life cycle of toxins. Pollution is released into the environment in the form of smoke and gases from combustion; exhaust fumes; and off-gasses from a variety of substances, such as vinyl and plastic. These pollutants, or toxic compounds, become trapped in the atmosphere. They remain there, mixing with the oxygen we breathe. They also combine with the vapors that form clouds. The rain that falls from the clouds contains a mixture of chemicals that then enters streams, rivers, oceans, and the soil. It is also present in crops, livestock, and fish. Humans, at the highest level of the food chain, are drinking polluted water, swimming and bathing in it, and eating foods that have been contaminated by it. The cycle continues and is compounded, as more pollution is released and the toxins already present continue their journey through the ecosystem.

### How the Body Deals with Toxins

Eventually and inevitably, toxins enter the bloodstream through the air we breathe, the water we drink and bathe in, and the food we eat. Studies have shown that the average baby is born with nearly 300 industrial contaminants in his or her body.[4] Understanding the impact of toxins on our physiology is critical. The human body is a finely tuned machine; its parts work in perfect concert to create overall harmony and well-being. Each system, organ, and cell of the body has a particular function; it collaborates with all the other parts and relies on them to do what they were designed to do. If any part is not functioning at its natural optimal level, every other part is affected.

Unfortunately, toxins disrupt the body's ability to function at its best, interrupting hormone production, metabolism, and dis-ease–fighting responses. Toxins literally get stuck in the body, stored in fat cells, bones, muscles, and organs. Disharmony and dis-ease result. Just look at the rise of dis-ease worldwide, including the increase of many cancers, diabetes, and asthma. Having this knowledge helps you see the importance of eliminating toxins from your life, wherever possible, by making healthier choices for your home and body. Unfortunately, we cannot always avoid coming into contact with toxins, so it is important to create a lifestyle that helps circumvent the effects of those that are already present.

## Where Did These Toxins Come From?

The Industrial Revolution was a time of great growth. It marked the beginning of innovative manufacturing processes that utilized machines powered by coal. One important development during this period was the large-scale production of chemicals. As technology advanced, the chemicals created began to multiply. Accordingly, the degree to which society was exposed to toxic chemicals increased. Furthermore, scientists and innovators looked only at the impact and perceived

benefits of each individual substance. Initially, there was very little research to determine if there were negative impacts on humans or the overall ecosystem. Additionally, no one took into account what would happen if these chemicals were mixed or came into widespread use (thereby compounding their effects).

By the 1950s, the standard philosophy was that chemistry created a better way of life. Through misinformation and distorted beliefs, it was accepted that products like infant formula could be fabricated in a way that made them far superior to their natural counterparts. This mindset continues today regarding household cleaning goods and other products that can be created in a laboratory. By 1958, only 8 of 12,000 chemicals were banned. Due to a lack of regulation, the proportion of chemicals created, allowed, and in use to chemicals banned remains relatively unchanged since the 1950s.[5] Consider this startling statistic from the book *Fundamentals of Integrated Design for Sustainable Building*: "Of the more than 80,000 chemicals registered with the Environmental Protection Agency, roughly 15,000 are on the market, and only a small percentage of these have been tested for human toxicity, and an even smaller percentage tested specifically for their effects on children."[6]

Our daily environments are filled with toxins that we breathe in, eat, or apply to our skin. The heavy burden of this cross-contamination obstructs the body's natural ability to function optimally. Unfortunately, laws to keep you and me safe are nonexistent. Thus, *you* are responsible for understanding what you bring into your home. You have the power to create a healthy living space for you and your family.

## Toxins Found in the Body

The Environmental Protection Agency studied a random sampling of the general population and discovered that the five most toxic industrial pollutants were found in the muscles, tissues, and bones of 100 percent of those sampled.[7] Industrial pollutants come from car exhaust pipes and smokestacks. Frighteningly, the indoor air quality of the average home is two to five times *worse* than outdoor air quality, as mentioned earlier.[8] So, what toxins are stuck in our muscles, tissues, and bones from *indoor* air pollution? As you will learn in the next chapter, many toxins that are absorbed into your body *stay* in your body unless you make a conscious effort to remove them. These toxins wreak havoc by interfering with your body's natural ability to run optimally, creating dis-ease.

Equipping yourself with the knowledge of what toxins are, where they come from, and how to decrease their effects is critical to maintaining great health and well-being. A full list of chemicals, their detrimental effects, and where they are found in your home is provided in Appendix A. Visit my website, www.christaoleary.com, for an even more extensive list.

### *Creating a Healthy Home*

When creating your healthy home, it is important to develop an awareness of what is and is not healthful. This can be exceptionally challenging amidst the deluge of tactics used to market products. Learning to decipher labels helps you gain the clarity to make informed

choices—moving you from habitual buying patterns to deliberate purchases based on knowledge. For now, we will look at a few of the most common toxic offenders.

Toxins are used in a wide array of products. A great example is volatile organic compounds (VOCs), which are found in plastic bottles, plastics in general (such as pacifiers, plastic straws, and cell phone cases), cleaning solvents, formaldehyde, benzene, alcohol, and pesticides. Another common form of indoor pollution is the radiation given off by electrical appliances, such as computers and microwave ovens; these emissions are called EMFs, or electromagnetic fields.

## Volatile Organic Compounds (VOCs)

Think about the following situation, with which you may be able to identify. You are excited to begin painting your bedroom. After looking at dozens of magazines, you discover the perfect color: a certain peaceful shade of blue. This weekend, you have set aside time to begin the process of painting the walls of your sanctuary. At the local hardware store, you navigate the displays of paint choices. You want the best and most healthful product for your home. You have heard that VOCs (volatile organic compounds), briefly mentioned above, are emitted from paint and are to be avoided due to their adverse effects on health.

Although there is greater awareness in recent years about VOCs, ambiguity still exists around what they are and the degree to which they impact health. Many people have no idea what the acronym stands for, and when they learn it contains the word *organic*, they assume it can't be that bad. However, "organic" in "volatile organic compound" only signifies that the substance contains carbon. "Volatile," on the other hand, sounds negative; but it just means that the compound evaporates easily at room temperature. Although VOCs *sound* like they should be healthful, you have learned that they are actually linked to cancer; respiratory issues; and damage to the liver, kidneys, and central nervous system. Arming yourself with this knowledge is the first step in creating your healthful home.

The second step is seeing through the deceptive advertising tactics of big business. Because you have done your research and are aware of the detrimental health effects of VOCs, you look for a paint that contains low or no VOCs. You find a shelf of base paint touting "No VOCs." Grabbing a few gallons, you bring them to the person in charge of transforming the base paint into your favorite color. You hand him the color sample you found in a magazine, as you daydream about how beautiful and healthy your bedroom will be. Not so fast! Unfortunately, when he starts injecting pigment (color) into the "No VOCs" base paint, he is *filling the can with VOCs* because, generally, most VOCs in paint are from the *pigment*. He hands you back the paint cans, which still say "No VOCs," and you leave thinking you are using something healthier than it actually is. It amazes me that companies can get away with these types of marketing ploys. The paint companies should have to tell you what is in the products you are actually bringing home.

Paint is big business. Seven hundred and fifty million gallons are sold annually. Of that, 10 percent ends up in landfills and waterways.[9] Ten percent may not

seem like a lot, but that's 75 million gallons of discarded paint, loaded with VOCs, going into the water we drink and bathe in and into the food we eat. For this reason, it is important to recycle paint and to use recycled paint products. The great thing about using recycled paint (but only paint manufactured after 1978, to assure it has no lead) is that as long as the recycling company does not introduce more pigment, the VOCs are naturally going to be lower because the product has already off-gassed a good portion of them over time.

VOCs can be found in a whole host of items for the home. I mentioned paint first because if you live in a house, chances are pretty good that there is paint on the walls. Another major issue with VOCs is that because they are present in such a wide variety of household products, our exposure to them has an increased, cumulative effect due to their high concentration. Other items that contain VOCs include cleaning products, hairspray, perfume, dry-cleaned garments, carpets, carpet pads, wallpaper, furniture, dye used in fabrics, and bedding and pajamas treated with fire retardants. With so many household items off-gassing noxious VOCs, it is important to be proactive in decreasing their impact—or to eliminate them, if possible.

I can offer some Home in Harmony Lifestyle quick fixes for removing VOCs from your world or negating their effects. First, determine where VOCs are lurking in your home. Next, begin to eliminate the items with VOCs. For example, choose organic pajamas for your family; find a hairspray that doesn't contain VOCs; and swap out cleaning products that have VOCs for truly natural ones, like vinegar and baking soda. Each time you eliminate an item containing VOCs, or exchange a product with a high level of VOCs for one with a low level, you decrease the concentration around you and its cumulative effect.

In recent years, homes have improved their energy efficiency through "air sealing." Sometimes, however, the sealing of air leaks produces a lack of adequate ventilation. Without proper ventilation, air becomes trapped in a home and continues to mix with pollutants—making air quality more and more toxic. It is especially important to ventilate sleeping areas, where you spend a lot of time, so try to let in fresh air. Plants are a natural air purification system. They actually clean toxic chemicals right out of the air. So, choose products wisely, throw open the windows, and incorporate plants! We will discuss more ways to counteract the effects of VOCs later in this chapter.

## Organic Solvents

Another group of toxic compounds whose name might fool you is organic solvents. Organic solvents are used to dissolve substances. They are derived from petroleum and, contrary to their name, are synthetic. Exposure to organic solvents (examples of which include toluene, trichloroethylene, and methylene chloride) disrupts your body's ability to function optimally, by suppressing the central nervous system. Organic solvents tend to accumulate in fat cells, such as breast tissue; indeed, the Breast Cancer Fund links breast cancer to organic solvents.[10]

Organic solvents can be found in a plethora of home goods, including cleaning products, glues, paints,

degreasing agents, fabrics, cosmetics, pharmaceuticals, and computer components. In dealing with organic solvents, as with VOCs, it is imperative to read labels and know what you are introducing into your home environment. As mentioned previously, ventilation is critical. Begin to take steps to clean the air in your house by using air filters, plants, zeolite crystals, and salt lamps, all of which will be discussed in more detail later in this chapter.

## Formaldehyde

Formaldehyde is another chemical found in numerous products for the home. When I think of formaldehyde, I remember science class and the stench emanating from glass jars of gross-looking things floating in liquid. (It's probably good that I didn't become a biologist.) The purpose of that smelly fluid, called formaldehyde, was to preserve the specimens in the jars by killing any microbes that would allow for natural decomposition. Formaldehyde is used in home products to kill bacteria that could damage the goods.

Unfortunately, the detrimental effects of this compound on your body are numerous. Formaldehyde is directly linked to cancer and is known to cause asthma, to damage DNA, and to depress the central nervous system.[11] According to sustainability expert Tracy Lydiatt, formaldehyde has been connected to "joint pain, depression, headaches, chest pains, ear infections, chronic fatigue, and insomnia."[12] Due to all of these negative health correlations, Japan has banned it from personal care products. Most countries, however, allow the use of formaldehyde, which is utilized in such diverse items as furniture, baby bedding, carpets, particleboard, furniture polishes, and skin care products. It is imperative to decrease your exposure to formaldehyde wherever you can, because it is so prevalent in our everyday lives. (You will find a list of chemical names associated with formaldehyde in Appendix A. For a more extensive list, go to www.christaoleary.com.)

## Perfluorinated Compounds (PFCs)

A healthy home requires nontoxic furnishings. Unfortunately, stain-resistant chemicals are toxic. As a mother of four, I understand how tempting it is to protect your new cushions, with their exquisite fabric, from the inevitable smudges, spots, and spills of daily living. However, when we begin to understand the toxic reality of our home environment, we realize it is more important to protect those breathing the air than to protect the upholstery. The perfluorinated compounds (PFCs) found in stain-resistant fabrics are known to cause cancer and are linked to developmental problems in children.[13] I suggest picking less expensive fabrics that do not contain stain-resistant chemicals—and accept that you may need to choose beautiful new fabrics more often.

## EMFs

I am personally very careful about EMFs in my household, because I feel that these electromagnetic fields around appliances wreak havoc on the body and brain. EMFs can create disruption in the nervous system,

causing conditions like depression, anxiety, and aggressive behavior. EMFs interfere with normal cell function and growth. This interference is associated with cancer, birth defects, headaches, and skin disorders. There are many medical studies refuting the possibility that EMFs have a negative impact on our health and well-being. Most of these studies, however, have been funded and published by the *source* of the EMFs. The power company doesn't want to admit that EMFs from high power lines have a detrimental effect on the body. This would create chaos in many communities where schools have been built under power lines because the land was cheaper.

I went around our house in Connecticut with a device that read EMF output. I was amazed at the distance that the EMFs carried. I tested the radiation from a microwave we seldom used and found that it projected at least six feet out when the appliance was on. We chose *not* to include a microwave in our current kitchen. Another source of EMFs is the alarm clock that sits next to your head seven or eight hours a night. Because of its close proximity, and the duration of exposure, it is one of the first things I would move or remove. Computers also emit EMFs. For a period each day, it is important to power down your computer—and "power up" your body with a walk *away* from the screen. The adverse effects of EMFs are magnified by length of contact. I will share more tips for dealing with EMFs later in this chapter.

The list of household toxins is long and includes substances like benzene, chlorine, and dioxin. I could write an entire book on this subject alone. My goal, however, is to help you begin the process of evaluating the products you are bringing into your home. Still, there are two more items I want to touch on in this chapter because they are either exceptionally common or we spend many hours breathing in their toxic off-gasses. They are mattresses and fragrance.

## Healthy Nest for a Good Night's Rest

You spend a large percentage of your day sleeping on a mattress. If you are like most people, your mattress is synthetic. More than likely, it is made of polyurethane foam, a petroleum-based product. Because synthetic mattresses are made of petroleum, they are highly flammable. Insurance companies actually refer to them as "solid gasoline." Due to the combustible nature of petroleum-based synthetic mattresses, manufacturers need to cover them with fire-retardant chemicals—which are toxic. Therefore, as you sleep, you are potentially breathing in noxious fumes from your mattress.

There are two things you can do to diminish the negative impact of your mattress. The first is to choose one made of an organic substance, like latex or wool. Natural mattresses are definitely more expensive but worth the price, to ensure that you are not being exposed to off-gasses for so many hours a night. If this is not an option, when you get a new synthetic mattress, throw open the windows and unwrap it, allowing it to air out for a number of days before you actually sleep on it. This practice helps diminish the impact of the initial off-gassing, although it doesn't prevent the evaporation of chemicals that occurs over the life of the product.

## Throwing You off the Scent

Fragrance inundates us everywhere we go; it is in so many of the products that literally touch our lives. First, take a minute to think about the word *fragrance*. What comes to mind? You might picture an advertisement for a designer perfume. I am a very visual person, so when I think of the word *fragrance*, I envision white sheets hanging from a clothesline, blowing in the crisp air with scents of lavender. In today's world, that image couldn't be further from reality. Nowadays, fragrance does not come from wide-open spaces or plant-based sources. Before the 20th century, fragrances were made from natural products—and there are still some out there that contain organically grown materials. However, according to the National Academy of Sciences, 95 percent of the compounds used to make fragrances are synthetic materials derived from petroleum or petrochemicals in a laboratory.[14] These chemicals are known to create dis-ease in the body. The Institute of Medicine puts fragrances in the same category as secondhand smoke.[15]

Fragrance is used in products from personal hygiene items to toilet bowl cleaners. There are even scented facial tissues and toilet paper! In our first home, I would put blue tablets in the toilet bowl to keep the commode super clean. (I admit I am a bit of a clean enthusiast.) Three months after we moved into our new abode, I became nauseous any time I entered the bathroom. About a month later, we realized I was pregnant. My body's instinctive response, designed to keep mom and baby safe, was that the tablets and their noxious fumes had to go. My very patient husband removed the blue water from the toilets so that I didn't have to go next door to use the facilities. I look back at that experience and marvel at the body's magnificent natural ability to keep us from danger. If only we were more in tune with the body—and listened to it.

Not only do we lather products with fragrance on us, allowing them to absorb through our skin, but we are bombarded with noxious scents when we walk into shops and other buildings. A few years ago, on a trip to Walt Disney World, we stayed at a big-chain resort. When I walked into the lobby for the first time, I thought, "Oh, this is lovely and peaceful. I feel like I am in a spa." I attributed my bliss to the fact that we had finally arrived at our destination, after a day of traveling with four children. But when I reentered the lobby later, I realized that the resort was pumping in fragrance to evoke a sense of tranquility. This marketing ploy is designed to get all the senses involved, so that guests will remember the experience and want to come back.

But I remembered the story of a project done by a middle school student for the California State Science Fair on the negative health impact of fragrance.[16] This girl sprayed cotton balls with brand-name fragrances and placed them in containers with live crickets. After only a matter of seconds, each cricket died. The only cricket to live more than 84 seconds was the one who did not have a cotton ball sprayed with fragrance in the container with it.[17] This experiment demonstrates the powerful effect of chemicals on living things. Despite any favorable thoughts we might have in association with the word *fragrance*, chemical scents are toxic. Yet we willingly fill our homes with them, falsely believing we are making ourselves and our environment cleaner or more sweet-smelling. It is time to wake up from the

misperception that these chemicals are not harmful and are acceptable to have in our homes.

A deceptive marketing tactic is labeling household products "fragrance free." Unfortunately, these products can still contain fragrance. The label just indicates that the products were created without a noticeable scent. In fact, neutralizing chemicals are used to *mask* scent—and manufacturers are not required to list chemicals used to conceal other fragrances. It is important to know how to read labels, so you can determine whether fragrances are lurking in the products in your home. It is also important to start listening to your body. Your sense of smell, especially, can be like radar—instantly knowing whether your environment is truly healthful.

## What to Do about Indoor Toxins

This section presents Home in Harmony Lifestyle antidotes to indoor air pollution, including air filters, plants, zeolite crystals, salt lamps, and techniques for avoiding EMFs.

### Air Filters

There are different types of filters that address a range of air quality issues. Some filters remove small particles from the air that can cause respiratory problems. Other filters help clean the air of toxic off-gasses that create dis-ease in the body. Utilizing both types of filters is best. To eliminate small particles from the air, I recommend an air-purifying system that has a high-efficiency particulate air (HEPA) filter. This kind of filter is especially important for those suffering from allergies or asthma. To eliminate the noxious off-gasses of VOCs,

organic solvents, and other harmful toxins, also employ an activated carbon (charcoal) filter.

*Plants*

Plants in your home provide an additional layer of filtration. Plants naturally purify the air, literally absorbing off-gasses and pollutants. Remember from science class that a plant takes in carbon dioxide ($CO_2$) and releases oxygen. This process re-oxygenates the air. Some plants are recognized for cleaning the air of specific toxins better than others. For example, the spider plant is known to filter formaldehyde, and the peace lily helps clear the air of trichloroethylene, a chemical found in dry cleaning. See Appendix A for a list of other plant-toxin combinations. For a more extensive list, go to www.christaoleary.com.

The best air quality results from using 1 potted plant per 100 square feet. So if your home is 2,500 square feet, you will want to include 25 plants in your interior design. If you live in a smaller space, you will need fewer plants. Of course, if you live in a 6,000-square-foot mansion, the number of plants required to absorb pollutants will be much higher. Plants can make your living environment not only healthier but beautiful.

*Zeolite Crystals*

Zeolite crystals are an additional way to clean the air in your home. Zeolite is a mineral composed of aluminum, silicon, and oxygen; it is often used as an absorbent. Zeolite crystals filter the air, remove odors, and absorb chemicals and harmful off-gasses. The crystals then release the pollutants they have absorbed and are recharged by placing them in sunlight. Using zeolite

crystals is a fabulous way to decrease VOCs and other toxins in your environment.

### Salt Lamps

Salt lamps are another means by which you can improve the air quality in your home. These hunks of mined salt, hollowed out to accommodate a light bulb or a small candle, help reduce pollutants and allergens. Like the ocean, they increase the number of negative ions in the air; these ions boost the immune system, increase energy, and relieve stress. The effects of salt lamps help counterbalance the negative impact of toxins.

### Avoiding EMFs

As mentioned earlier, harmful EMFs emanate from man-made products such as televisions, computers, microwaves, fluorescent lights, and electric blankets. The detrimental impact of EMFs is increased with time spent using appliances that give off this electromagnetic energy. That being said, in today's world, it is hard to imagine *not* utilizing, or completely avoiding, devices that emit EMFs. So you might ask, "What can I do?"

For starters, create an EMF-free—or at least EMF-low—zone in your bedroom. The average person spends six to eight hours in the bedroom each day. Minimizing the EMFs in this area will help decrease your overall exposure. Furthermore, while you sleep, your body is in a mode of renewal and recovery; exposure to EMFs during this phase doesn't allow for optimal restoration. So, first remove the electric clock on the bedside table. Replace it with a clock that does not produce EMFs. Also, stay away from electric blankets that emit EMFs. Finally, for best results, unplug everything in your bedroom before you go to sleep. Elsewhere in your home, begin to notice your proximity to and usage of appliances such as microwaves, computers, tablets, cell phones, and fluorescent lighting. Creating distance between you and these devices and unplugging them for a time will help reduce the damaging effects of EMFs. Place ferns next to appliances, if possible, to help keep some of the EMF waves from reaching you.

Ultimately, the key to creating a healthy home is a conscious awareness of the products you bring into it. When beginning this journey, it is easy to feel overwhelmed. Therefore, it is sometimes simpler to just ignore the toxic reality and revert to old habits. However, remembering the truth about what toxins are, what they do to your body, where they are lurking in your life, and how they are marketed gives you the power of choice. Keep in mind that manufacturers are in the business of selling things, no matter how healthful they are. Take time to question products and read labels. Like learning to walk, this task can feel insurmountable; but each new decision contributes to the momentum of designing your healthy home. You have already taken the first step, by choosing to read this book. Your initial few steps will build confidence, inspiring subsequent steps, until you have created your Home in Harmony Lifestyle.

### Creating a Sacred Space

Our home environment has an impact on every aspect of our well-being. It touches us physically, mentally, and spiritually. It either drains our energy or

nurtures our essence. You are affected by such qualities of your home as clutter, color, and furniture positioning. It is time to understand how your living environment impacts you and how you can make it a sacred space that supports your well-being.

One idea to keep in mind is that our homes "talk" to us. It is important to become aware of what the objects in your home are saying to you. Each item is continuously sending messages to your conscious mind and to your subconscious. Maybe the jar filled with shells you collected on your last beach vacation reminds you of frolicking in the sea, or the antique rug given to you by a recently deceased loved one reminds you of your fresh grief. The stories associated with your decor either boost your energy or deplete you.

Often, we have walked by an item so many times that we have forgotten about our positive or negative connections with it. But our unconscious remembers. An example might be the beautiful lamp Aunt Sally gave you years ago. Unfortunately, since receiving the gift, you had a falling out with Sally. Right after the disagreement, when you walked past the lamp, it reminded you of your hurt feelings. Now, years later, you are no longer conscious of those feelings. Yet your subconscious hasn't forgotten, and every time you are near the lamp, it depresses you. Conversely, you can use the communication property of objects to affirm something into your life. For example, you might place symbols of your dreams or aspirations in your home, to help manifest these experiences. I have a fountain in my office that continuously reminds me that Spirit is flowing in my life. This thought, conscious or unconscious, uplifts me every time I hear the cascading water or see its graceful flow. Again, everything in our homes talks to us on some level, so it is important to notice the messages you are receiving. Make sure everything that surrounds you lifts your spirit.

## Clutter

If you walk into your house and see piles of clutter, you will feel deprived of vitality. In contrast, if you come home to a well-ordered haven, you will feel rejuvenated and able to face the challenges of everyday living. Think about an area in your home that is in disarray or disorganized. It might be a drawer, a closet, or a room. Ask yourself how this space makes you feel. When I think about clutter that I need to tackle, my shoulders sink and I feel defeated. Clutter weighs down the body, mind, and spirit. Unfortunately, even if we become blind to the clutter, our subconscious is aware of it—which dampens our vitality. Clear the clutter so that your home can recharge you to meet the demands of the outside world.

## Color

Color is fascinating. It affects us on every level. Color symbolizes and means different things in different cultures. For example, in the United States, white is associated with purity and innocence; therefore, it is the color of classic weddings. In China, on the other hand, white is connected with the death ceremony. Not only do colors have significance from a cultural perspective, we often have our own personal perceptions of them.

It is important to understand your relationships with various colors so you can utilize ones that nourish you. I don't love purple. It took me a while to recognize where my disdain for this color came from. I remembered that when I was a young child, my mom would coax me to take a horrendously distasteful asthma medicine that was purple. To this day, whenever I see that color, I immediately feel queasy. This understanding allows me to consciously abstain from using purple in my home because it would not support me. Aim to utilize colors in your environment that create the most favorable conditions for you.

Studies have shown that color affects our physiology and psychology. For instance, blue is scientifically proven to produce a cooling effect on the body (physiology) and a calming effect on the mind (psychology). Let's look in more detail at some psychological responses to color and how these responses correlate to feng shui.

Returning to blue, this color is a favorite for many people; in fact, it is the color most preferred by men. That may be one of the reasons my husband always loves my decorating . . . I use blue everywhere! In our Cape Cod home, every wall except in the girls' room has a different shade of blue paint on it, ranging from Benjamin Moore's Blue Dragon to Soft Sky. Blue creates a feeling of serenity. When designing a space that is intended to be tranquil, I choose blue tones. Blue is also said to bring clarity and focus to a person's thinking. Therefore, it is a great color to incorporate into an office setting. Physically, blue lowers the heart rate and body temperature. It also decreases a person's appetite. Thus, it is a good color to use in your kitchen if you are struggling with weight issues. The only instance in which blue is not recommended is when a person is feeling depressed, because blue can exacerbate feelings of loneliness and sadness. That being said, begin to notice how the color blue affects you personally. Does it cause you to sigh with contentment or feel a twinge of "the blues"?

Red is the universal color of passion. In feng shui, red is correlated with aggression, anger (as in "seeing red"), and increased energy. The names of certain shades of red and phrases with the word *red* in them have a primal, fight-or-flight quality: "blood red," "fire engine red," "red alert," "red hot." In ancient societies, as well as today's, red is a symbol of status, power, and virility. Think of the red "power tie" and the red carpet. Physiologically, red increases the heart rate and appetite. Begin to notice how restaurants, especially the large chain establishments, incorporate red into their interior design. Red stimulates hunger and encourages conversation—which is perfect for a dining room but not so good for a bedroom or main living area. If people in your home tend to become easily agitated or confrontational, you might calm their temperaments with a cooler palette. Observing how the color red impacts your mind and body will help you design your environment.

With the often frenetic nature of our lives, it is no wonder that many people embrace earth tones. The earthy palette includes colors like tan, taupe, and brown. These hues fill the pages of magazines and have a grounding effect on the mind and body. They convey a sense of stability, orderliness, and permanence. Earth tones are great to use in a bedroom or in a room with cathedral ceilings, to help you feel rooted and nurtured in your space. Avoid brown, however, if you have low energy and find yourself sitting on the couch most of

the day. Again, choose colors that will have the best effect on your overall well-being.

Yellow is cheerful and "sunny." Words associated with yellow include *happy, bright,* and *active.* Yellow is uplifting and energizing. It stimulates the nervous system and activates memory ability. Yellow also encourages communication and increases mental sharpness. It is a great color for kitchens and family rooms because it promotes clear conversation and social interaction. I had a client whose goal was to get her teenage boys to engage more. They had fallen into a routine in which they would fly into the kitchen, grab something, and go. She visualized her boys coming in, sitting down, and having lovely and lively discussions. Accordingly, we chose to paint the room yellow. We also incorporated a brown couch, to encourage the boys to sit for a while instead of using the kitchen as a takeout restaurant. A few months after completion, she called me; through "happy tears," she told me that the boys would actually sit down with her and have a bit of family time. This is just another example of how colors impact your life.

Green evokes feelings of balance, healing, and freshness. It is no wonder that television studios use this color in the waiting area ("greenroom") for guests and performers before they go on air. Green is also associated with expansion, abundance, and prosperity. Of course, green ink is used to print U.S. currency. Incorporating green into your decor can help you feel balanced and energized.

Cultural associations with white, introduced earlier, run the gamut from purity to death, clarity to weakness. Understanding your own ingrained response to white will help you determine whether to use it in your sanctuary. If white signifies new beginnings, clarity, innocence, or purity for you, go ahead and integrate it into your environment. If you have more negative associations, however, you should replace white with a more supportive color.

Black is another color with a wide variety of correlations. On the one hand, it can be considered a "power color"—strong, commanding, and ominous. It is also associated with death, moodiness, and depression. In addition, it can be linked to secrecy and mystery. I would avoid black when you are feeling down or unheard. Knowing what your connection to black is will help you determine whether to include it in your home.

## Placement

The placement of objects in a room plays a dynamic role in how the space feels. You can position furniture to create an environment that best fortifies you. The first step is to become aware of whether you need to feel more grounded in your space—or you require a bit more energy. The answer will suggest whether you need a more balanced environment, in order to feel more centered—or you require an asymmetrical space that will spice things up.

Think of symmetrically placed objects like items of the same weight in the two pans of a scale—balanced. Symmetry is grounding and calming. In contrast, asymmetry (lack of balance) adds excitement and surprise to a room. I had designed a very balanced room for a show house in Connecticut. I kept the proportions of various objects similar; used pairs of items; and employed

a serene palette of blue, gold, and white. The result was a grounded sense of peace and harmony. I felt that the room needed a little more energy, though, so I included artwork and flowers, which were completely unbalanced, on the mantle. This touch added whimsy to the space and helped it become featured in publications across the country. Knowing what you need from your sacred setting will give you the first clue as to how you should position furniture and other objects within it.

Here are some additional guidelines for the placement of furniture and other objects in your home.

### Bed Position

As mentioned earlier, bed placement is important to getting a good night's sleep. It is best to position the bed *away* from the door, oriented so that those who enter your room are in your direct line of sight. In this way, your instinctive fight-or-flight response is not unconsciously triggered. I will share more about bed position later in this chapter.

### Dining Spaces

When choosing a table, determine the *goal* of your dining space. Round tables promote conversation, and rectangular tables create a hierarchy. Your position *at* the table has an impact on your sense of harmony. To feel calm, take a seat from which you can see the entire room, or at least those coming toward you. This will ensure that your hard-wired system for reacting to threats is not on alert, thereby creating a low level of constant anxiety. Think of gangster movies, in which the characters sit with their backs to the wall for protection.

### Desk Placement

Put your desk where you can see the door. Having your desk in this position allows you to concentrate on the task at hand. Otherwise, your brain naturally focuses, in part, on what may come up from behind you. This instinctive process is based on the drive for survival. Unfortunately, it prevents you from getting as much done as you could. Being unable to fully focus on your work projects can have a broader impact on your life, so make sure your desk is in a favorable position.

### Comfy Couch

A couch is only comfy if you can fully relax on it—that is, when your fight-or-flight instinct is not being activated. To ensure restfulness, place your couch against a wall. If this is not possible, put a sofa table behind the couch to create a subconscious barrier to wide-open spaces, which make us want to flee.

## Discovering Feng Shui

My dear mother-in-law once described me as a seeker of knowledge. I was younger at the time and didn't quite see myself that way—but I thought it sounded cool. She had witnessed a pull that drew me to seek an understanding of people, my environment, and the purpose of life. I read anything I could on subjects that intrigued me and took classes and seminars on many interesting topics that seemed to have no connection to each other. I would take a sharp left because a particular subject seemed compelling and then take a hard right because another subject made sense and appeared to hold so many answers. Fortunately, my internal navigation

system would course-correct and bring me back to a balanced place, allowing me to absorb the vast expertise and wisdom of hundreds—sometimes thousands—of years. My openness to accept and embrace so many varying systems helped me create a life of well-being. I integrated these schools of thought into a lifestyle that I wholeheartedly believe in, live, and am sharing with you.

I spent seven years absorbed in the study of psychology. The theories, and the lives of the individuals who conceptualized them, fascinated me. I wanted to know what compelled these psychologists to study behavior, human interactions, and the brain. Maybe their lives held some special key to happiness. Looking back, I can see I was trying to make sense of my own upbringing—to understand why only some people were satisfied with their lives, and to ensure that I would be one of them.

Fortunately, I never found the answers I was looking for, and I continued my search (although, back then, I didn't realize it *was* a search). Around the time we built our second home, I became intrigued by the teachings of feng shui. After years of studying from a Western psychological perspective, I was a bit skeptical about this ancient Eastern view. Nonetheless, it piqued my curiosity. As I read feng shui texts, I carried out small experiments to see if there was validity to the principles presented.

One such experiment took place a few months after we moved into our new home, where I had designed every little detail, right down to the doorknobs. If you have ever built a house, you know that it can be a very expensive endeavor, especially if you want it appointed exactly to your liking. My husband and I had always loved to travel and would take a number of vacations each year, along with monthly weekend getaways.

When we were in our previous home, our neighbors had jokingly referred to us as the "renters," because we were *away* more than we were home. When we moved to our new home, our budget was tight; there was more house to manage, and we didn't seem to get away like we used to. Missing our excursions and adventures, I decided to see if I could use "this feng shui thing" to jump-start our traveling again.

I did some research and found the part of the house that feng shui correlates with travel. It happened to be in our study, which was located at the front of the house, some distance from the main living area. We were purposely using this space as a temporary repository for unpacked boxes and artwork that we hadn't had a chance to hang yet. One of the basic premises of feng shui is that clutter should be cleared. Indeed, every time I walked past this particular room, I felt angst at its disorder; it was draining my energy, and my frustration introduced negative vibes into our living space and lives. At once, I began to clear the boxes and find spots for the artwork. I decided not to mention my experiment to my husband, waiting to see what—if anything—happened. Within a few weeks, my husband came home from work and announced that he had to take a business trip to France—and it might be fun and romantic for me to meet him there for an extended weekend! He had already talked to the sitter, and she was more than happy to stay with the kids. Needless to say, this little test increased my interest in feng shui. How did it really work? I brought an array of books on feng shui to keep me occupied on my six-hour flight to Paris.

## The Complementary Lenses of Psychology and Feng Shui

As I began to delve deeper into the studies of feng shui and interior design, I realized that good design typically had a natural state of feng shui. That is, when you walk into a room and it feels good, the space usually has a harmonious use of color, positioning, and proportion—reflecting principles of both feng shui and interior design. This sense of balance is perceived by our internal feedback system, which is purely instinctual. It is the same system that, in psychology, engages our fight-or-flight response. In other words, we have an innate need for a safe, supportive, and nurturing environment that facilitates our survival. When you are in a space that is out of balance, is cluttered, or has awkwardly positioned furniture, your inborn feedback system is activated. This system sends messages to the brain that you are unsafe or need to be on alert. From a physical perspective, these messages trigger the secretion of cortisol, the body's stress hormone. Cortisol is known to diminish clear thinking, increase weight gain, and create dis-ease in the body. It is one thing if you briefly visit a space that is out of balance. If you *live* in an unbalanced environment, your cortisol is triggered continuously—which can have a major impact on your overall well-being. I will share a personal example of this phenomenon.

When my son was in the first grade, he began to experience disturbances in his sleep. This was odd because he had always been a great sleeper. Initially, the incidents were small, but they quickly escalated. On one particular evening, he awoke wide-eyed, screaming, "Get them off of me! Get them off of me!" He was standing on his bed, yelling like this. Then he jumped down and sprinted, at full speed, in the direction of his windows. Thankfully, I was close enough to block him, but his velocity and determination knocked me off my feet. My husband was able to contain him while I called the pediatrician. In a total panic, through a stream of tears, I told him what had occurred. In his Irish brogue, our sweet, older pediatrician gently explained, "No need to worry. He is just having a night terror. These can come and go, but most young'uns outgrow them."

I was relieved that this seemingly bizarre and frightening behavior could be explained. However, I was unable to simply stand by until the next episode took place. Over the course of a few months, and with the guidance of our beloved pediatrician, we sought out specialists and endured numerous brain scans and sleep evaluations. In preparation for these sleep studies, we attempted to keep our son up all night so he would then be able to sleep in a lab while hooked up to machines, with onlookers observing his every twitch (yah, right!). On another late night, we awoke to his terror-filled screams and the sound of running. I caught him just as he attempted to jump down a full flight of stairs in his effort to get away from whatever was "on him" in his panicked dream state. The next morning, delirious, I turned to feng shui for a solution.

My son's room was one of my favorites. I had really gotten creative with it, because I wanted him to love it and to transition effortlessly to it from his room in our previous home. His bed looked like a wooden dinghy (small boat). The lower portions of the walls were painted blue, like the sea; a border of waving nautical flags appeared at the horizon. Additional authentic Coast

Guard flags in vibrant reds, yellows, and blues adorned the walls. At one end of the room, a train table was set up, loaded with wooden trains, tracks, and stations. The bed was positioned close to the door. This bright and cheery space was very inviting and enticed one to play—but it didn't foster sleep or a sense of relaxation.

As I began to assess the room through the lens of feng shui, I recognized the many mistakes I had made. Then I experienced an "aha moment": The ancient practice of feng shui was in complete alignment with the principles of psychology. The two schools of thought had many commonalities with regard to our behavioral responses to the environment. These responses affect every area life, including family dynamics, achievement at work, health, and the ability to sleep well.

It was time for a makeover. I felt like an artist who was repainting a picture despite liking the original. I embarked on redesigning the space using a new set of tools (feng shui) as well as an old paradigm (psychology). I had not previously realized that psychology was important in creating a supportive environment. First, I needed to address the stimulating colors: hydrangea blue, fire engine red, and sunburst yellow.

As I pointed out earlier, the color red encourages feelings of aggression and anger. It also promotes movement and activity. Feng shui associates red with the "fire element" and recognizes it as a stimulant, which helps move stagnant energy. Feng shui also suggests that using too much red in a space can have a negative impact by promoting excitability. As mentioned before, red increases heart rate and hunger. Needless to say, the qualities associated with red are not exactly optimal for a bedroom or a place where people rest. Rather, red is more conducive to social spaces. Again, it is an appropriate color in the design of a restaurant because it encourages conversation and stimulates appetite—but you may want to avoid it in your kitchen if you struggle with weight issues.

In the redesign, I chose calming and grounding colors. I painted the walls the color of sand. I removed the red window valances (short curtains that decorate the top of a window) and went with heavy, navy, full-length panels. These draperies gave the area a sense of weight, permanence, and supportive strength. To make the space feel like a boy's room, I incorporated bronze baseball finials. Bronze contributed the sensation of timelessness. The combination of soothing colors (sand, navy, and white) created a comforting environment that would be conducive to restorative activities like reading and sleeping.

According to feng shui, the "command position" in any room is a powerful spot. In the bedroom, the principle of command position dictates several things about the placement of the bed: The bed should be as far from the bedroom door as possible, allowing the widest view of the room; when lying on your back in bed, you should be able to clearly see the door; and the bed should *not* be in the direct path of the doorway. From a psychological and physiological perspective, this placement makes perfect sense! If an intruder were to enter, being able to see the door would give you an opportunity to react. If you couldn't see the door, you would have less reaction time. Our primitive ancestors slept in caves, positioning themselves so they could watch the entry. This instinct for self-protection is embedded in our DNA. If your bed does not have a full view of the door, your fight-or-flight

response is triggered—stimulating the subconscious into a state of readiness that hinders your ability to get restful sleep. This continuous tension and stress, although subconscious, triggers the release of cortisol, mentioned earlier in the chapter. Cortisol interferes with the nervous system and the body's restorative abilities. The resulting interruption to your sleep has an impact on your overall well-being. I know that I need sufficient *restful* sleep in order to function at an optimal level.

I reevaluated the position of my son's bed according to the principles of psychology and feng shui. I moved the bed from the wall the door was on to a wall where he could have a commanding view of the door and the overall room. The goal was to allow my son's brain to move from an unconscious state of heightened activity to a relaxed state that would allow restorative sleep. In that vein, I replaced the vibrant nautical flags with calming art. My son's beloved trains were moved to the playroom, where active diversions were encouraged. I placed a big brown suede chair in a corner to give the room a sense of grounding, support, and strength and to be a spot for the soothing activity of reading.

These changes made the space peaceful and promoted rest. Upon entering the room, you would immediately take a deep breath, relax your shoulders, and feel the release of tension. You were drawn to the big brown chair and cozy blanket, enticing you to curl up with a good book. The change was palpable. But what interested me most was that the night terrors disappeared! I paused to process the fact that our environment has a huge impact on our lives—and we can manipulate it to create the life of our dreams.

## Harmony in Action

For the next seven days, do the following:

1. Notice which colors excite and inspire you and which ones you find distasteful and unpleasant.

2. Clear the clutter from one small area of your home.

3. Notice which toxic items in your environment you could swap out for healthy options.

Your home environment plays an important role in your physical, mental, and spiritual well-being. Creating an inspired, healthy, and vibrant home lays the foundation for an inspired, healthy, and vibrant *you*. Developing awareness around the products you bring home—that is, whether they are healthful or toxic—is the first step in radiant living. The second step is designing a sacred space that fosters your intentions for your life. Recognizing that your home plays a profound role in your existence—one that can deplete your vitality or support you in all ways—is a foundational element of the Home in Harmony Lifestyle. In the next chapter, we will talk more about toxins—those you bring into your body.

## Chapter Three

# The Second Pillar: A Healthy Body

The second pillar of the Home in Harmony Lifestyle is a healthy body. Being healthy is paramount to leading a vibrant life. This chapter gives you a blueprint for optimal physical well-being. We will take another look at toxins, including what they are, where they are, and their full impact on your body. You will then arm yourself with healthy choices that can help you achieve radiant health.

### Toxic Body

Toxins are a sobering part of our daily lives. They are so prevalent that it often seems easier to ignore them than to deal with them. This phenomenon is sometimes

called the "ostrich effect": You bury your head in the sand rather than listen to the inconvenient truth. Toxins and their devastating effects have so permeated our lives that the idea of finding and implementing solutions can be overwhelming. My hope is that after we discuss the impact of toxins, you will be motivated to take action. I will make this process easier for you by providing simple steps to transition from living in a toxic soup to enjoying a nontoxic lifestyle.

Regarding the ostrich effect, I am reminded of a day at the playground years ago. I had just begun to make the connection between the chemicals in our food and the toxins in our environment. I had spent countless hours deciphering labels to make sure I wasn't bringing home any products containing milk or milk-protein derivatives. Again, this vigilance was critical in order to keep my son from having an exaggerated allergic reaction. (I had personally witnessed Bailey's lips turn blue from lack of oxygen at his first drop of milk when he was nine months old. The terror of this experience was beyond comprehension for me as a mother.) As I began to learn the toxic truth, I wanted to share this information with as many moms as I could. I was certain that if *they* knew what *I* did, they would make healthier choices for their families. Wrong!

On that day at the playground, we were with our playgroup, which met once a week to socialize the kids and give the parents a chance for grown-up talk. One of the moms pulled out a juice box for her child. I knew from my research that this particular item contained a whole host of toxic ingredients. I excitedly began to describe what was actually in the juice, starting with the substance that made it red. I explained how there had been studies connecting red food dye to malignant tumors in lab mice. I thought for sure this information would be embraced with enthusiasm. Wouldn't every mom want to know if she was giving her child something harmful? The woman looked at me skeptically, as if to say, "They wouldn't sell it in a grocery store if it was harmful to people." She stuck the straw in the box and handed it to her child. This was one example of many where it was easier—more convenient and less scary—for someone to put his or her head in the sand and ignore the facts.

## Government Regulation of Toxins in Food

To make conscious choices about what you bring home, you need to know where toxins are lurking. Manufacturers practice marketing gimmicks that make this difficult to assess. Only a handful of regulations protect consumers, and there are so many loopholes that manufacturers, not consumers, have the upper hand. I am intrigued by how other countries handle toxins. I am saddened to know that the United States, in comparison to many other countries, has looser regulations regarding chemicals and toxins. The United States isn't protecting its people and the environment, holding manufacturers in higher regard.

The abundant toxins in our food include trans fats, additives, preservatives, pesticides, hormones, antibiotics, petroleum, coal, mercury, lead, and other heavy metals. Many ingredients "approved for use in our food supply by the U.S. Food and Drug Administration . . . are banned in other countries who find sufficient supportive

evidence to link the ingredients to detrimental health effects."[1] Believe it or not, it is sometimes the *packaging* of food that contains toxins. As an important example, the synthetic compound bisphenol A (BPA) is used to line cans, in order to keep the metal from corroding and to prevent the food from becoming contaminated by bacteria. Unfortunately, BPA from the lining leaches into the canned goods. Studies show that low doses of BPA have a negative impact on health.

## Food Toxins and Dis-ease

We need to be aware of the toxins in our food. We really are what we eat! Unfortunately, the toxins we consume in food wreak havoc on our bodies. The impact is evident in the increased levels of dis-ease in our culture.

The probability rates for cancer speak volumes: "41.24% of men and women born today will be diagnosed with cancer . . . at some time during their lifetime. This number can also be expressed as 1 in 2 men and women will be diagnosed with cancer . . . during their lifetime."[2] The link between toxins and cancer is recognized. According to the National Cancer Institute, "Researchers have estimated that as many as two in three cases of cancer (67 percent) are linked to some type of environmental factor, including . . . exposures to radiation, infectious agents, and substances in the air, water, and soil."[3] The President's Cancer Panel updates the U.S. president regularly regarding the National Cancer Program. This panel, which includes eminent scientists or doctors, reported to President Obama in 2010 that "the true burden of environmentally induced cancers has been grossly underestimated."[4] Environmental factors, including exposure to carcinogens, are said to be responsible for at least three-quarters of cancer diagnosis and death in the United States.[5] In fact, "About 6 percent of cancer deaths per year—34,000 deaths annually—are directly linked to occupational and environmental exposures to known, specific carcinogens."[6]

The obesity rate has jumped and continues to rise; currently, more than a third of U.S. adults are obese.[7] The prevalence of asthma increased 75 percent between 1980 and 1994[8] and has continued to climb since then.[9] The incidence of food allergies among children increased 18 percent between 1997 and 2007.[10] The number of Americans with diabetes is expected to hit an all-time high of 15 percent by 2015, equating to more than 37 million Americans.[11] These figures are staggering! But they make sense when we consider what we are consuming.

It is difficult to ignore statistics. Let me give you an example from my own experience. In 1998, I was sitting on the floor of a friend's playroom, in her finished basement. We were watching the kids in our playgroup crawl around and grasp at each other's toys. I was surrounded by eight mothers who ranged in age from their late 20s to early 30s. We started to discuss breast cancer and the shocking fact that, at the time, one in eight women would get breast cancer in her lifetime. Again, back then, that was a scary statistic. I would have preferred to ignore it as I looked around and realized there was a good chance that one of the eight beautiful women in the room with me would get breast cancer. A little over ten years later, that statistic became a reality. In a two-month span, both my mother and one of my dearest friends, who had been part of that playgroup, were

diagnosed with breast cancer. A few years later, another woman in that group was also diagnosed with cancer. These were people who exercised, paid attention to their weight, and ate what the FDA deemed healthy. At that point, I realized I needed to get the message out about what was really in our food and environment.

We can no longer afford to put our heads in the sand and ignore the toxins that pervade our daily lives, impacting our health and the health of generations to come.

### Creating a Healthy Body

To understand the detrimental impact of toxins on your body, it is important to appreciate the body as a system. This awareness will let you see the connection between toxin-free living and vibrant health. Then you can make truly informed choices for yourself and your family. In this section, we will also discuss additional strategies for stepping away from toxins and moving into a cleaner, more healthful lifestyle.

## The Body as a System

It is amazing to think about how the body actually works, how all the organs function in perfect harmony. It is even more breathtaking to ponder the flawlessly coordinated processes that take place on a cellular level every day. Most of the time, we take this beautiful orchestration for granted—but the thought of it is profoundly inspiring.

It is necessary to look at the body as a system made up of subsystems that must all be functioning properly in order for health to be achieved. Understanding that each system relies on all the other systems is key. If one system shuts down or malfunctions, all the other systems are affected. When I explain this to my kids or to seminar participants, I usually use the analogy of a car. If one part of a car is not working correctly, it affects the way the car drives. For example, if a wheel is out of alignment, the car goes out of balance, and it takes more energy and effort to stay on course and get to your destination. The same holds true for the body. If one part is malfunctioning, it throws the entire system out of balance. The body can continuously make adjustments to correct the imbalance, but this effort puts stress on the parts of the system that are trying to compensate for the malfunctioning part. Unfortunately, this strain can eventually create dis-ease in the body.

When discussing the body and toxins, it is important to understand that each physiological system has an intake function and an elimination function. At this point, you might be wondering why it is necessary to learn about bodily function and systems within systems. I don't blame you. As I mentioned earlier, it is probably a good thing I went into a creative career (design) rather than biology. However, that being said, even I believe it is important to understand how toxins affect the body. Otherwise, it is too easy to ignore the toxic truth.

So, every organ and every cell take in energy to run and then eliminate anything they see as waste. The waste moves through the body and is eventually excreted. This process occurs for the largest of organs and the smallest of cells. Waste is eliminated when we exhale, sweat, and

urinate, but the majority of waste material is excreted through the colon (large intestine). If the elimination ability of any system is blocked, a domino effect backs up the entire system. Disruption, stagnation, and disease result.

Part of the problem is that, generally speaking, people are consuming much less fiber than is necessary to keep their systems running smoothly. Jim Lonzo, senior nutritionist at Kripalu Center for Yoga & Health, recently spoke at a seminar I attended called "Good Gut, Good Health." According to Lonzo, the average American consumes only 10 grams of fiber a day, because the S.A.D. (standard American diet) consists of processed foods, hydrogenated oils, and refined sugars. This amount is nowhere near the 30 to 40 grams recommended by nutritionists. Lonzo explained that we are descended from Paleolithic hunter-gatherers whose staples, seven million years ago, were nuts, berries, fruits, veggies, and protein. This diet gave them an estimated 100 grams of fiber a day. In the Neolithic Era, agriculture was introduced. Farming changed the types of foods that were consumed and the amount of fiber that was ingested. Lonzo states that we are genetically predisposed to the Paleolithic diet, and the change to the Neolithic diet or to a more modern diet has created digestive problems, including constipation, that affect overall health.

The colon is the body's main avenue for eliminating waste and unwanted materials, such as the toxic debris left over from fumes we breathe or food we ingest. Due to the amount of waste processed through the colon, it is imperative that this organ be working optimally. When it malfunctions, everything from weight to vitality is affected. According to the American Society of Colon and Rectal Surgeons, 80 percent of the population suffers from constipation at one time or another.[12] If the colon is unable to eliminate toxic sediment, it becomes trapped in the body. It has no way of getting out! The accumulated toxic waste is then absorbed into our bones, muscles, fat, and organs, because it has nowhere else to go. Depending on the data you look at, the average American stores between 8 and 25 pounds of impacted fecal matter in his or her colon. This undigested matter holds toxic debris that is absorbed by the body if it remains in stagnation due to constipation.

This stagnant mass also takes up a great deal of space. The large and small intestines are approximately 25 feet long. The large intestine sits next to virtually every major organ in the body. A swollen mass of stagnant fecal matter taking up extra space within the body cavity can have a detrimental effect on the function of every organ the colon touches—impacting the health of the larger system. If the swollen colon is taking up room where the lungs are, for example, it becomes difficult for the lungs to function optimally—making it hard to breath. All of the organs that are being crowded by a swollen mass of fecal matter will fail to operate optimally. I know how gross this sounds, but it is imperative that your body is able to effectively eliminate waste.

## Toxins and Weight

Toxins are an unfortunate part of our lives. When you take your head out of the sand and really begin to assess the magnitude of your exposure to toxins, it can be very overwhelming. Realizing that toxins are in our

outdoor air, our indoor environments, the foods we consume, the water we drink, and the lotions we rub on our bodies is scary. Even more alarming is that these toxins become trapped in our systems, causing weight issues, hormonal disruption, and dis-ease.

Toxins have a detrimental effect on weight in a few ways. The systems of the body are perfectly orchestrated to keep us alive, first and foremost. If we are cut, for instance, the body sends specific cells to help ward off infection and coagulate the blood. If you ingest something that has spoiled, the body eliminates it to keep you alive, making you vomit or giving you a bad case of diarrhea. This "keep you alive" system similarly kicks in when toxins enter the body. The body's focus becomes dealing with the invading toxins. All energy goes toward flushing them out—instead of toward flushing out fat. In other words, the body must get rid of the toxins that are trapped *in* fat cells before it worries about getting rid of the fat cells themselves. Because of the inundation of the body by toxins, the system becomes overworked and exhausted. The end result is a slowing down of the metabolism and an inhibition of the natural processing of food.

I have a fascination with anything that affects the brain and then impacts behavior, which is one of the reasons I love the study of psychology. Toxins play a role in how the brain functions, which subsequently influences behavior. This concept is important in discussing the impact of toxins on weight. Toxins actually disrupt the ability of the stomach to communicate to the brain that it is full. The toxins interfere with or block these important messages, which can result in overeating and weight gain.

Another side effect of toxins is their impact on the key organs involved in metabolism. Specifically, the liver becomes overworked and sluggish. The liver is the main filtration system for the body. It metabolizes drugs, detoxifies chemicals, and filters the blood coming from the digestive tract. Like the anti-virus program on your computer, it is the protective "wall" that doesn't allow toxic debris into the system—debris that could shut down the entire system the way a virus might corrupt a computer. You must continuously update your anti-virus program to be able to deal with new viruses that might attempt to enter your computer. Similarly, it is critical to clean and maintain your liver so that it is able to function optimally without becoming overwhelmed. Otherwise, metabolism will slow, contributing to weight gain—or worse, toxic debris will enter the system, potentially creating dis-ease.

## Toxic Body Burden

If I haven't said it enough, I will say it again. Toxins are all around us. We are living in a toxic soup. To repeat a stunning statistic presented earlier, the Environmental Protection Agency did a study on industrial pollution and found that 100 percent of those sampled had the five most toxic industrial substances in their bodies.[13] These chemicals and others create disharmony and dis-ease in our systems. It is important to become aware of this toxic truth. Then it is imperative to move from living unconsciously to making empowered choices that support your well-being.

Due to inundation by toxins, many people have what is called "toxic body burden." This term refers to the total quantity of toxic substances stuck in cells, bones, muscles, and fat. Research shows that the average person has over 700 contaminants in his or her body.[14] The Environmental Protection Agency did a human tissue survey that found chemicals in the fat cells of 100 percent of those sampled.[15] This study demonstrates that we are all affected by toxins. It is no wonder that cancer rates continue to rise, the incidence of asthma has skyrocketed, diabetes is expected to increase dramatically, and more and more children are suffering from food allergies.

In my research, one particular study poignantly illustrated the concept of how toxins become trapped in our systems. Before the 1970s, the chemical DDT was widely used as a pesticide. For those old enough to remember, planes were shown on television spraying crops with DDT. In 1972, DDT was banned under the Stockholm Convention and prohibited from use in the United States. Scientists in Michigan sampled four-year-old children in 2006—34 years after the use of DDT was halted—and found DDT in their bodies. They surmised that the mothers of the children had been exposed to food products containing DDT nearly 35 years earlier, and the toxins had become stuck in their tissues and fat cells. The toxins were then released from the tissues and fat cells into the mothers' milk during breast-feeding.[16] It is hard to fathom that toxins could become stuck in someone's body for over 30 years. This story exemplifies the impact of toxins on so many levels.

# How to Deal with Toxins

The statistics on toxins can be very frightening. When presented with a scary situation, your options are to turn away and pretend it isn't true (because that would be too terrifying) or to look at it head-on and figure out how to deal with it. My plan is to arm you with the tools you need to face the toxic reality and manage it. In brief, here is my plan for handling toxins in food:

1. Be aware that toxins are found in many foods.

2. Learn to decipher food labels for misleading claims.

3. Take action to reduce the toxins in your body.

These measures will move you from a state of fear-based inaction to empowerment and responsive execution. This shift is critical in addressing toxins and in implementing the Home in Harmony Lifestyle.

*Knowledge Is Power*

The first step in finding healthier solutions is becoming aware. Being conscious of what is going on around you allows you to make informed choices. Giving yourself options puts you in the driver's seat: You are able to decide what you want in your life and what you don't. Although this new-found awareness can be alarming, it is time to see clearly. The truth gives you the power of decision—based on fact, not fiction.

*Deciphering Deceptive Labels*

The next step in dealing with food toxins is learning how to see through the deceptive marketing tactics used in labeling. It amazes me how manufacturers in many industries are allowed to mislead consumers and how stronger regulations aren't in place to protect the average person. It is important to become aware of this sad truth so you can make knowledgeable decisions about the products you bring into your home.

When I refer to deceptive marketing practices, I am talking about claims made on labels that products are "green" or "all natural." Unfortunately, there are no laws regarding these specific terms, and companies use them as an advertising tactic. The same holds true for the label "free-range" as applied to products of meat, egg, and dairy farming. When I see an item called "free-range," I picture open fields, with animals roaming and grazing. Then I snap myself back to the reality that this term only signifies that the animals had some access to the outdoors each day. Otherwise, they could have lived in substandard, overcrowded, and unhygienic conditions. That being said, there *are* farmers out there who go above and beyond the existing industry standards to grow and nurture products that would meet an aware person's criteria for healthy food. I want to applaud their ideals and practices. Unfortunately, these extraordinary individuals are the exception, not the rule.

Another deceptive labeling practice is claiming that a product has "no additives" or "no chemicals added." Consider this scenario: You maneuver the grocery store to the cereal aisle. You pick up a box that reads "no additives." You assume that you are about to bring home a healthful product. Not so fast! This label only means that no chemicals were added to the box of cereal you are holding. However (and this is a big "however"), the ingredients used in *producing* the cereal, such as grain, might have been immersed in toxic chemicals. As long as the manufacturer did not physically add chemicals to the end product, the label "no additives" can be used. In other words, regulations *allow* that box of cereal to contain additives or chemicals that were included earlier in the process.

These are just a few of the misleading marketing ploys allowed by law. (For additional examples, go to www.christaoleary.com.) Unfortunately, these sorts of practices are permitted in the marketing of not just foods but beauty products and furniture, to name a few things. Deciphering deceptive labels will help you create a healthier home and body.

*Reducing Toxins in Your Body*

Now that we have faced the scary truth, let's begin to look at ways to clean up the mess. This step involves learning how to remove built-up toxic debris from your system. Detoxes and cleanses seem to be all the rage right now. You might hear that celebrities are doing them or that someone you know thinks they are a quick way to lose some extra weight. The truth is that detoxification programs *are* a great way to remove toxins from your system; they can also make you look and feel great and can have a huge impact on weight. Imagine shedding the ten pounds of extra fecal matter we discussed earlier! When you start to release this impacted sludge from your colon *and* remove the toxic debris from your system, imagine how efficiently and effectively your body will begin to operate. Eliminating these life-draining

impediments allows your body and all of its systems (including metabolism) to come back into balance and to function at their natural optimal levels. (Before you embark on a detox or a cleanse, please remember to ask your doctor if it is appropriate for your body.) Removing toxins that have been stuck in your cells for years and years is one strategy for creating good health.

Another solution is to sweat those chemicals out! Exercise offers so many benefits. It increases the release of serotonin (the "happy" hormone that improves mood), helps cardiovascular (heart) health, increases metabolism (which helps with weight loss), *and* removes toxins from the body! Taking 30 minutes a day to *break a sweat* helps your body release accumulated toxins. This activity could be anything from walking briskly to dancing in your living room. (Go to www.christaoleary.com for other exercise suggestions.) Exercising to the point of sweating is fundamental to the Home in Harmony Lifestyle.

To summarize, conscious awareness lets you determine what to bring into your home—and what to get rid of. Learning to decipher gimmicks and deceptive practices in labeling is another important part of making informed and healthful decisions. Selecting chemical-free foods, furnishings, and other products is a big move forward in creating a healthy body and home—leading to a lifestyle that nurtures your overall well-being.

The next step is to learn about amazing whole foods you can incorporate into your life to promote vibrant health. I believe so strongly in the restorative benefits of these foods that I have dedicated an entire section to them. We will look at which foods you should include in

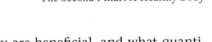

your pantry, why they are beneficial, and what quantities you need to consume in order to see results.

## *Superfoods*

We have talked about the negative effects of consuming toxic foods, but eating the *right* foods can have an incredibly positive impact on the body. A clean-eating lifestyle not only supports the body but creates optimal health. Marketers often tout the importance of dis-ease–fighting foods. One day, it's red wine; the next day, it's goji berries. This section will help you sift through the deluge of information and will answer some of the most common questions about "superfoods": What are they? Why are they good for you? How much do you have to eat to gain their benefits? In Appendix B, I will share some simple recipes to help you incorporate superfoods into your wellness lifestyle.

It might surprise you to know that for most of my life, I was unaware of the impact of food on my body— except whether something would give me big hips or thighs. I was excruciatingly conscious of my curvy frame starting at a very young age. Echoes of my older sibling calling me "thunder thighs" and "jelly belly" rang in my ears for years. I developed a love-hate relationship with food. Many people resonate with the frustrations of yo-yo dieting and a lack of willpower around food. These experiences and feelings become cycles of pain, creating low self-esteem and an unbalanced relationship with food.

I didn't realize that the issue was the *types of food* I was eating, not *how much* I was eating. I craved sweet,

salty, and fatty foods. Ingesting these types of foods threw my system out of balance—creating more cravings and inhibiting my metabolism. When I was in middle school and high school, in the morning, I would have Pop-Tarts, which were loaded with sugar and other chemicals. If I was making my own lunch or dinner, I would opt for Chef Boyardee canned ravioli or an entire packet of fettuccine Alfredo. In the summer, I thoroughly enjoyed starting my day with a large chocolate-chocolate-chip muffin, washed down by diet fudge soda. A friend recently reminded me that the majority of evenings on our summer breaks from college were filled with creamy clam chowder; fried, whole-belly clams; and beer. At the time, I didn't recognize these foods as the reason for my lethargy, nausea, and stomach pains.

The notion that every cloud has a silver lining holds true more often than not. And when we can't see the silver lining, it's probably because we don't have a full understanding of the situation. Such was the case with my son's milk-protein allergy. At the time, the thought that a drop of milk or a hidden ingredient in a jar of baby food could send him into anaphylactic shock, an allergic reaction that may cause death, was beyond frightening for me. Spending countless hours examining labels, researching ingredients, and searching for alternatives was exhausting. Now, 15 years later, I look back and am thankful for the experience. It gave me the opportunity to expand my understanding of food, the food industry, and the chemicals that inundate our world. Without the experience of my son's food allergy, I would never have awakened to the clean-eating lifestyle that supports our family on every level.

I was one of those kids who didn't do something I was told unless I fully understood *why*. This was definitely true for food. I can remember my grandmother trying to convince me to eat spinach. I wanted to know why. She explained that it made Popeye strong, and if I wanted to be strong, I needed to eat it. At the time, I really didn't want to look like Popeye. I decided to press my grandmother's spinach theory further. I asked her, "How much spinach does someone need to eat to be strong like Popeye?" I don't think I ever got an answer, and I don't remember ever eating spinach when I was young. I needed concrete evidence of the benefits *before* eating something that looked as unappealing as spinach packed in a can. Although I do thoroughly enjoy spinach today, I still need to clearly understand the touted health benefits of a food before I will integrate it into my diet.

## What Is Clean Eating?

There are various schools of thought regarding clean eating, but my approach is simple: If a whole-food item was grown in the ground and has not been tampered with (sprayed, treated, or injected with toxic chemicals), it is considered a clean-eating food. When I say "whole food," I am referring to grown foods that remain as close to their natural state as possible. Because so many products line the shelves of grocery stores, I find it easiest to put them in five categories. These categories form a continuum from unhealthiest to healthiest, from toxic to superfood:

| TOXIC | TOXIC RISK | UNNECESSARY | HIGHLY RECOMMENDED | SUPERFOOD |
|---|---|---|---|---|
| Processed, filled with sugar and chemicals | Grown from the ground but chemically treated | Organic but processed | Organic | Organic and nutrient-dense |

Begin to notice where the items in your cart fall on this continuum. A boxed, processed food filled with sugar and chemicals goes in the "toxic" category. A food that has been grown in the ground but has unfortunately been treated with chemicals is placed in the "toxic risk" category. A processed food with the organic seal ranks higher on the health scale but is deemed "unnecessary." Foods that are grown in the ground and have the organic seal are classified as "highly recommended." The "super-food" category is reserved for those organically grown foods that are so nutrient-dense they are in a league of their own. These are the foods I want to share with you.

I am going to present 11 superfoods that I would recommend incorporating into your Home in Harmony Lifestyle. (For a more extensive list, go to www .christaoleary.com.) I will let you know how much of each superfood to include in your diet and provide alternatives with similar properties and health benefits, just in case you want to vary what you eat or don't care for the original item.

## Blueberries

Let's start with blueberries. I often tell audiences about a conversation I had with an old friend I hadn't seen in many, many months. We were enjoying a girly day of lunch, shopping, and a trip to a beautiful spa. I sat on the side of the hot tub, wrapped in a luxurious white robe, with my hair pulled back in a bun and my feet dangling in the bubbling, warm water. My friend looked at me with a perplexed expression. "What?" I asked. In a serious tone, she responded, "How is it that you don't have any wrinkles? Do you get injections in your forehead?" I laughed and answered, "It's because I eat my blueberries!" I went on to explain the incredible benefits of blueberries, from their ability to promote collagen production (hence, no wrinkles)[17] to their antioxidant and anti-inflammatory properties. I also explained how they can reverse degenerative dis-eases associated with memory loss[18] and are a great source of fiber. It is easy to incorporate a cup or two of blueberries into your day by throwing a handful on your morning yogurt or including them in a smoothie. If you aren't crazy about blueberries, you can substitute cranberries, raspberries, strawberries, or cherries. I am often asked what to do when these berries are not in season. I plan ahead and stock my freezer!

## Broccoli

My family actually races to get heaping second helpings of my simple broccoli sauté. This delights me because I know my loved ones are receiving so many amazing health benefits from these green florets that are considered one of the most nutrient-dense foods available. (You can find my easy recipe for sautéed broccoli in Appendix B.) My girls will ask me to make an egg scramble with sautéed broccoli in the mornings before they head to school. I always comply because I know it

strengthens the immune system, builds bone strength, and boosts cardiovascular health.[19] Eating just half a cup of broccoli a day creates these benefits. If broccoli isn't a favorite in your house, you can use turnips, cauliflower, or bok choy for the same health benefits.

## Spinach

My grandmother was right: We should all eat our spinach. Consuming just one cup of cooked spinach or two cups of raw spinach daily lowers your risk for many cancers, cataracts, and cardiovascular dis-ease; it also gives a boost to the aging brain.[20] If you feel about spinach the way I did when I was young, include romaine lettuce, kale, or collard greens in your salads, sautés, and smoothies instead.

## Flaxseeds

Flaxseeds are easy to incorporate into your diet because you can sprinkle them on virtually anything. I put a heaping tablespoon in my morning protein shake, which helps balance the estrogen in my body. Flaxseeds are high in protein, which helps me feel full; and high in fiber, which helps my system run smoothly. They contain magnesium, iron, potassium, and omega-3, an essential fatty acid. Crushed and ground flaxseeds are more bioavailable than whole flaxseeds, which means the body can digest them and absorb their nutrients more easily.

## Tomatoes

Tomatoes do a whole host of positive things for the body. I am going to mention two that amaze me. First, they protect against cancer because they contain the free-radical-fighting antioxidant lycopene.[21] Second, they increase the skin's ability to tolerate sun exposure without getting burned![22] Interestingly, processed tomatoes, as found in pasta sauce, salsa, and ketchup, are more bioavailable than fresh tomatoes. This is the only time I will suggest incorporating a processed product into your healthy lifestyle. It is important to include a few servings of tomatoes and processed tomatoes weekly and to increase that amount in the summer when you will be spending more time outside. It's wonderful that nature blesses us with an abundance of tomatoes during the season when our bodies need them most.

## Salmon

Salmon is high in omega-3, which helps build healthy cells and helps lower the risk of many dis-eases including or associated with cancer, heart health, memory loss, asthma, and insulin resistance.[23] I highly recommend choosing wild-caught salmon over farm-raised salmon or (worse) genetically engineered salmon. Genetically modified salmon, dubbed "frankenfish," grows two to three times faster than wild salmon. Both engineered and farmed salmon are raised in fish farms; because of their large numbers, they are given antibiotics to prevent dis-ease. So again, incorporating salmon into your diet is important, but you must choose the right kind. If

you don't have a fondness for this pink fish, both halibut and sea bass also contain omega-3. Including two to four servings of fish rich in omega-3 per week can create lasting health benefits.

## Quinoa

Quinoa is a staple in our home. It is one of those easy foods that I make in bulk at the beginning of the week and then add to salads and soups or enjoy plain. Quinoa is packed with protein and contains *twice as much fiber* as other grains. It also has iron, which promotes red-blood-cell health and increases brain function.[24] In addition, quinoa contains the antioxidant manganese, which fights the free radicals produced when we are exposed to toxins and keeps them from damaging our red blood cells. Eating one cup of quinoa daily provides an impressive amount of nutrients. Interestingly, quinoa is considered a seed, not a grain. If quinoa is not palatable to you, I recommend substituting a whole grain that is high in both fiber and protein.

## Beans and Lentils

I love whipping up a great bean dip that I can toss on a salad, use as a spread, or scoop up with vegetables. (You can find a few of my favorite bean recipes in Appendix B and at www.christaoleary.com.) Bean dip is another one of the dishes that I make in a large quantity at the beginning of the week to have on hand. I love beans because whatever form you eat them in, they have a big impact. They keep you feeling full because they are a low-fat protein with a slow-burning energy release that helps stabilize your blood sugar. They are also high in fiber, which helps your body run efficiently and effectively. In addition, beans contain lignans, which help decrease the risk of estrogen-related cancers like breast cancer.[25] To gain the maximum benefit from beans and lentils, consume one of the many varieties (pinto beans, chickpeas, great northern beans, cannellini beans, lima beans, green peas, or snap peas, to name just a few) at least four times a week.

## Tea

As I mentioned earlier, I was once a coffee drinker. Actually, I took coffee consumption to the level of addiction. That being said, I totally understand if you are a fan of coffee and cringe at the idea of sipping tea. However, when you read about the amazing benefits of tea, you might be inclined to change your habit. One cup of tea (brewed green or black, not instant or herbal) daily gives you fluoride to help fight cavities. It also has flavonoids, which lower your risk for osteoporosis and cancer.[26] Additionally, drinking tea can help decrease wrinkles[27] and prevent skin cancer.[28] I find it interesting that old wives' tales often have merit. Such is the case with the idea that drinking tea when you have a cold or the flu will help. Indeed, tea has antiviral, anti-inflammatory, and anti-allergy properties. Maybe you can swap one of your daily cups of coffee for a nice mug of brewed tea.

## Eggs

When you experience the sensation of a craving, what is happening on a physiological level is that the pancreas—the blood sugar regulator—is communicating to the brain that it needs glucose. You may reach for a cookie, which will lead to the fast release of glucose in the body. However, due to the speed of this process, you will be reaching for another cookie sooner rather than later. Choosing a protein, like an egg, to satisfy a craving gives a *slow* release of glucose into the system—helping you feel satiated longer and inhibiting further cravings. Eggs are considered to possess the perfect balance of amino acids, and they contain all nine of the amino acids that aid in cellular repair. Eating an egg a day supports eye function and increases the body's ability to fight carcinogens from the environment and food.[29] I find it easy to have a few hard-boiled eggs ready and waiting in my refrigerator when cravings hit. Eating an egg helps me stave off hunger—and lets me incorporate a nutrient-dense superfood into my diet.

## Avocados

I eat at least one avocado a day. Not only are avocados delicious on salads or chopped up with hard-boiled eggs, they are a great source of fiber and support the body in a number of ways. They decrease inflammation and are said to help arthritis.[30] They also support cardiovascular health, lowering the risk of heart disease.[31] Avocados help the body absorb nutrients at an optimized level[32] and promote blood sugar regulation[33]—assisting with

weight control.[34] New research has shown that avocados have anti-cancer properties that help cancer cells move into a state of apoptosis (the process of cell death).[35]

These are but a few of the abundant superfoods nature has given us. Again, Appendix B includes simple recipes to help you incorporate superfoods into your daily routine. These dishes are fresh, easy to prepare, and packed with nutrients. It is time to acknowledge what you are putting into your body and how it is making you feel. Assessing the foods you consume is the first step in adopting a clean-eating lifestyle. Creating positive habits from informed, conscious choices lets you design your inspired life!

## Harmony in Action

For the next seven days, do the following:

1. Notice how often you purposefully sweat for at least 30 minutes.

2. Notice where the items you regularly consume fall on the continuum from toxic to superfood.

3. Notice how often you are moving toxins through your body by having a bowel movement.

Great health puts you in a position to be an active co-creator in every aspect of your life. To attain or maintain

optimal health, you must understand the nature and magnitude of toxins, steer clear of the avoidable ones, and flush out the ones that are already in your system. In creating a healthy lifestyle, it is critical to learn how to read labels and be aware of the marketing tactics employed by food manufacturers. Finally, incorporating nutrient-dense superfoods into your diet encourages your body's peak function. As you implement these simple solutions, you will move toward attaining the healthy body that is the second pillar of the Home in Harmony Lifestyle. Next we will discuss how to achieve balance on another level—the mind.

*Chapter Four*

# The Third Pillar: A Calm Mind

A calm mind is the third pillar of the Home in Harmony Lifestyle. In our fast-paced world, we are constantly trying to find calm in the midst of chaos. We *naturally* seek peace, our inherent state of equilibrium. In this chapter, I will explain how to use habits to create mental harmony and balance. We will examine the impact of today's omnipresent technology on your overall sense of well-being and how you can unplug from this psychological and physiological stressor. Finally, we will discuss the benefits of meditation so you can appreciate its potential impact on your mind.

### The Power of Habit in Creating Calm or Chaos

In our hectic world, it is becoming increasingly important to find ways to create inner peace. I want you to picture a small boat on the open sea, attempting to

sail through a powerful storm, with waves crashing on the deck. Be honest: Isn't this a fairly accurate metaphor for the turmoil of your mental state much of the time? This chapter aims to steer your mind from turbulent waters to the sanctuary of a quiet harbor.

The first chapter of this book was dedicated to noticing and evaluating habitual patterns in your life. Since reading that chapter, I hope you have begun to gain an awareness of your own habits. Bringing thoughts, words, and actions to an observable level can provide valuable insights into your behavior. In terms of inner peace, keep in mind that many typical habits are culturally acceptable but *create chaos* in people's lives.

To move from the churning currents of chaos to the still port of calm, start by examining your habitual patterns in the following foundational areas: your thoughts, your relationship to technology, your relationships with people, your eating and exercise routines, and your home environment. Your habits in these five areas can have a *huge* impact on your well-being. Always remember that you have the power to choose which habits you want to keep (the ones that support you) and which ones you want to replace (the ones that undermine you).

## Your Thoughts

Your thoughts create your reality. In other words, the way you think about life determines your experience. One person looking out a window might see a big, scary world and feel panic; another person looking out the same window might see a magnificent vista and feel awe. Their perceptions are different, so their experiences are different. Related to this dynamic, an interesting phenomenon occurs: We often draw experiences to us that prove our thoughts are accurate. Some people call this "self-fulfilling prophecy," while others call it the universal law of attraction. Whatever you call it, it's important to examine the lens through which you view the world. The way to get a handle on this ingrained viewpoint is to begin noticing the things you repeatedly say to yourself throughout the day. Are these messages positive or negative? Do they focus on lack or abundance? Are they things you heard as a child that no longer serve you? Begin to notice these habitual thoughts, and replace the damaging ones with uplifting ones. You have this power.

## Your Relationship to Technology

Over the last 20 years, technology has truly infiltrated our lives. In our search for internal stillness, it is necessary to examine technology's hold over individuals and over society. Take a moment to think first about inner peace and then about technology; notice how the images and sensations connected to the two ideas are contradictory. Later in this chapter, we will look more thoroughly at the impact of technology on our well-being. In the meantime, begin to assess your relationship to technology. Start to become mindful of your interactions with it and any habits you have around it. What are the implications of your technology-related habits? Do they interfere with your ability to find calmness?

## Your Relationships with People

There are times in your life when you need to release habits that deplete your vitality. These habits might relate to toxic food, clutter in your living environment, negative chatter in your head, or *people who drain your energy*. When we begin to notice our behavioral patterns, we can identify the life-draining individuals in our worlds. Toxic interactions with others sometimes become entrenched habits. You can actively choose to disengage from these unconscious dances. To create inner calm, it is vital to remedy unhealthy patterns in our relationships, releasing individuals who sap our essence.

## Your Eating and Exercise Routines

As previously discussed, the foods we ingest have a tremendous impact on our overall well-being. Begin to notice your relationship to food and your habits surrounding it. Are you eating things that support your health and create vitality? Or are you consuming items that diminish your health and create dis-ease? Do you habitually grab a snack without taking time to notice what your body truly needs—if it needs anything at all? You must become a conscious participant in your diet in order to find inner harmony.

The importance of exercise was mentioned earlier, in the chapters on habits and creating a healthy body. Exercise is also a fundamental part of finding inner peace. When beginning the journey from chaos to calm, it is helpful to look at the role of exercise in your life. Exercise is a natural way to "inject happiness" into your day when things are looking bleak. When we exercise, the hormone serotonin is released into the bloodstream, sending the brain messages of joy. I find that when I am having a difficult time with something, going out for a walk or a good run consistently improves my state of mind and gives me a fresh perspective. As mentioned earlier, I have taken advantage of the principles of habit formation to establish a regular behavior (putting my sneakers on when I go out to the bus stop) that facilitates my exercise routine. Physical movement grounds me as I begin the majority of my day's activities.

## Your Home Environment

An inspired home is the first pillar of the Home in Harmony Lifestyle because your living environment has such a big impact on your sense of calm, harmony, peace, balance, and well-being. The choices you make in your home, whether conscious or habitual, contribute greatly to the vibrancy of your life. Removing unneeded items from your home gives your mind breathing room, relieving you of the burdensome weight of disorder. Incorporating items that support you is critical to self-care; this nurturing habit prepares you to go out into the world and be the best you can be.

Let's look more closely at what the items in your home are communicating. As covered previously, everything in your living space talks to you. See and hear the messages. Do the objects that surround you on a daily basis send you supportive, nurturing messages—or life-draining ones that exhaust your vitality? For example, when you walk by the piece of art you picked up on a

recent vacation, it makes you smile. As time goes by and the artwork fades into the background, your subconscious still takes note of the happy memories; your spirit is uplifted whenever you pass it. The same phenomenon occurs when you are in the vicinity of an item that holds *negative* associations. For instance, the expensive vase that was a gift from a relative who made unkind remarks to you when you were young triggers those draining mental impressions in your subconscious every time the piece comes into view.

## Gratitude

When speaking of creating habits that support you, I would be remiss if I didn't mention gratitude. We often hear people talking about the ills of the world, the negative things that have happened to them or to others. Becoming aware of these conversations is critical to finding inner stillness. As discussed earlier, your thoughts about the world create your reality. Continuously focusing on negative situations and people is limiting and draining. Step out of this toxic pattern and direct your attention instead to what you are thankful for. Start your day by noticing five things for which you are grateful. This regular practice helps ground you in positive energy and serves as a catalyst for finding inner harmony. My hope is that you can begin to replace any unfavorable thoughts about your life with thoughts of gratitude. Then watch how the habit of gratitude attracts more things to be grateful for into your life.

As your day unfolds, identify your habits and assess whether they bring you up or down. Clear the aspects of your life that have become stagnant, creating dis-ease and inhibiting inner peace. Based on these efforts, all areas of your life will begin to shift. Let the current carry you gently to the calm of your inner harbor.

## Technology and Its Effect on Your Happiness

Let's look more closely at the role of technology in moving from chaos to calm. The growth of technology in the last few decades has been staggering. Both children and adults have become addicted to smartphones, portable music and video players, tablets, computers, televisions, e-book readers, and other technological inventions. People often seem to be attached to their electronic devices, whether they bring their cell phone to dinner; listen to their portable media player as they ride the bus; or fall asleep with their tablet on their lap, waiting for the next instant message to come in. This section describes the psychological and physiological impacts of technology and can help you determine your level of attachment—or addiction.

Are the technological appliances in your life constructive tools—or appendages? To clarify this distinction, I will ask you to reflect on some questions and perhaps embark on a few challenges. When I pose these questions, I want you to notice if you feel them in your body. Your body is a big antenna for reading all sorts of things, including people, situations, your feelings, and your emotional state. It sends you signals that can help you evaluate your life. For example, the hair on your

arms might stand up in a scary situation; your heart might pound in a stressful scenario; or you might have "butterflies" in your stomach when you are nervous. Visceral reactions (such as constriction of your throat, sweaty palms, or heaviness in your chest) to the upcoming questions could be very telling about your relationship with technology and its effect on you.

I challenge you, as you read this section, to remain fully present in your body and be aware of your thoughts. Sometimes when we don't want to hear something, we "tune out"—we don't listen, or we let our attention wander far away, to a place disconnected from our physical body. Living in an unconscious state like this can become the norm, especially when we are facing tough questions and situations. Again, as you go through the next few pages, check in with your body and your thoughts. Are you zoning out because the information makes you uncomfortable? Is your heart racing because you resonate with the observations being made? Stay tuned in to your internal messaging system.

## Your Attachment to Technology

*Question: What would happen if you left your cell phone off for an extended period?*

Of course, "an extended period" is relative. To me, an extended period without my cell phone might be the better part of a day. To my grandfather, it might be a week. To my son, a few hours might seem like an eternity. At 15, my son experienced two negative events in one weekend. While we were sitting in the emergency room, waiting for the doctor to stitch up the gash in his forehead from an accident at the gym (which had also caused a concussion), he said to me, "Ah, Mom, this has really been a bad weekend. First, I lose my phone while fishing—and I don't even like fishing. Now I have a concussion and a cut, so I can't play lax [lacrosse] for the rest of the season. This really sucks. I can't even text my friends to tell them what happened." I wasn't sure if he was more upset about his lost phone or the injury that prevented him from playing a sport he loved. My guess was that his missing phone was having the greater impact on his angst at the time. I really didn't want to know the answer, so I didn't ask.

Bailey ended up being without his phone for two days before the replacement arrived. To him, it felt like forever. Our experience of time in relation to technology varies greatly. Begin to notice where you are on the continuum. What would it feel like to unplug for a portion of your day? Consider testing your willingness—and ability—to disconnect. Can you go to the grocery store without your phone? If you are worried that someone in particular wouldn't be able to reach you in an emergency, you can give that person the store's phone number. When thinking about this challenge, do you feel it in your body? Or are you zoning out, contemplating the ten e-mails you need to send? Your reaction to this challenge gives you a big hint as to your level of technological attachment.

## Absence from the Present Moment

*Question: Do you stare into your smartphone instead of experiencing the present moment?*

A few years ago, we were at a sporting tournament for one of our children. Throughout the weekend, we enjoyed the company of many friends we had come to know quite well through the kids' sporting endeavors. Weekends like this allowed us to bond as we shared the camaraderie of team spirit and parenthood. Throughout the weekend, my girlfriend was constantly texting, often breaking out into laughter at one funny message or another. By dinner on the second night, we had started calling her "CrackBerry." In her defense, she was texting one of her children, who had not come along on the trip. She explained, "You'll see, when your kids get to this age, it's a great way to keep tabs on them and stay connected."

Almost ten years later, this phenomenon is so widespread that you often see patrons in restaurants with cell phones next to their plates so they won't miss that important text or call. As a culture, we are so consumed by technology that instead of being present in the moment, fully enjoying the food on our plate or the company of the person sitting across from us, we divide our attention between the technological world and the here and now. This split leaves us feeling scattered and unfulfilled. My children play sports on different fields and rinks, and I am often driving them around to different locations, so I understand the need to keep tabs; but I am also aware that communicating with them excessively would take away from my ability to be truly present. Although I have personally been scolded at our favorite lobster shack on Cape Cod, I am thankful for the sign that hangs there as a reminder to be in the moment—eating good food, hanging out with friends, and savoring the summer. It reads, "No texting or cell phones! That means you, idiot."

## Technological Inundation

*Question: How much time does your child spend in front of technology a day? How much time do you spend in front of technology?*

According to a *New York Times* article, Americans spend eight hours a day in front of various technological screens.[1] This screen time has psychological and physical effects on young and old. Recently, my two middle-school girls were in our yard playing one-on-one lacrosse. The game became more than a little bit tense, and I heard yelling. As I looked out the window, one child was chasing the other, stick raised high. The ball was no longer part of the equation! I looked beyond the flying ponytails and noticed my good-natured neighbor out on his deck trying to conduct a business call.

The next morning, as I walked my little one to the bus stop, I paused to apologize to our neighbors for the girls' outlandish behavior the day before. They were outside, the husband about to take his wife to work at the elementary school down the road. All night, I could only imagine what this schoolteacher was thinking about how we were raising our competitive, aggressive, and very physical kids—especially because they had raised three beautiful, polite, sweet girls who sometimes babysat for our children. To my shock and relief, they both exclaimed, "Christa, there is no need to apologize! If anything, we are always so happy to see your kids outside whether it is in nice weather or the middle of

winter." They continued, "We drive around the neighborhoods and are always so disappointed that no children are outside playing. It is wonderful to see them outside and to hear them playing."

I walked away, relieved of my embarrassment. But what my neighbors said made me think. It's true: Children are spending less time outside enjoying imaginative, inspired, and unstructured play. One consequence is that rates of childhood obesity and diabetes are on the rise. According to *The Daily Green*, a publication of GoodHousekeeping.com, kids spend nearly 55 hours a week in front of technology.[2] Their lack of physical activity has detrimental effects on their weight and overall health.

For adults, the cost of inundation and overstimulation by technology has many facets. The incidence of obesity in adults, as in children, has increased due to a sedentary lifestyle. Further, the pace of our lives has begun to mirror the rapid rate of technological change. We must multitask, overwhelmed by the myriad pressures of daily life—work responsibilities, volunteer commitments, parenting, household duties, and social commitments. The speed with which technology allows us to communicate makes our lives even more frenetic. We can receive phone calls, text messages, and e-mails 24 hours a day, and we are able to respond right away. One might think this convenience would make us more efficient and effective. What it actually does, however, is create an environment of stress—sending the stress hormone cortisol coursing through the body. This elevated cortisol is the natural response to the flight-or-fight instinct that keeps us alive during situations that are perceived as attacks. Physiologically, our energy increases, allowing us to run faster and farther if necessary to survive. However, this natural reaction was intended to be a *temporary* state. After the initial surge of cortisol, the body is designed to return to equilibrium. But this doesn't happen when we are expected (by ourselves or others) to respond immediately to requests for our attention. Unfortunately, the stress that has resulted from technological advancement strains the body and its ability to flow in a natural state of balance. Stress affects both physical and mental performance, blood pressure, immunity, and even weight! It is critical to set aside time each day to unplug from technology and take a deep breath.

## Disconnecting from Technology

Begin to evaluate how much time you spend connected to technology. What is your reaction to the thought of purposefully unplugging for a period each day? The answer indicates how attached (or addicted) you are. As you take small steps to unplug from technology, your levels of overwhelm and stress will start to go down. I suggest that you refrain from using technological devices an hour before bed, to help decrease your cortisol levels and improve your sleep quality. This measure will dramatically enhance your overall sense of well-being. Turn off technology at mealtime, to be fully present while you are nourishing yourself. You will be more conscious of the signals your body is sending. This elevated awareness can have a positive impact on your weight. Additionally, unplugging from technology frees you up to engage in other activities, like exercising,

enjoying the outdoors, or partaking in an uplifting pastime. Moving your body, breathing fresh air, and participating in joyful activities help decrease cortisol and stress.

Before moving on to the next section, please ask yourself again whether technology is a tool or an appendage for you.

### Inner Peace Through Meditation

For some, the word *meditation* conjures up images of gurus in white robes, wearing turbans and sitting on pillows amidst candles and incense. Although there are people in the world who meditate this way, it is not remotely the only option. You can choose from a variety of meditation formats. What if you were able to meditate while sitting at your desk, which produced inspired ideas and dramatically improved your productivity? What if you could find an inner stillness and peace that helped you move from chaos to calm in *all areas of your life*? In this section, we will look at numerous ways to incorporate meditation into your lifestyle—and recent scientific studies that show why you should. We will examine why meditation is beneficial not only to your mind but to your body and spirit.

## What Is Meditation?

There are many traditions and schools of thought regarding what meditation is and how it should be done. I like to look at the merits of each approach and identify which techniques resonate with me personally.

Similarly, I often tell my kids not to accept someone else's idea, statement, or belief as truth without assessing it for themselves—does it feel right to them? If you look at a particular type of meditation and it doesn't line up with your beliefs, move on and find one that does.

Meditation is the act of focusing one's attention on the present moment and filtering out any superfluous external stimuli. This practice allows the mind to rest from the chaotic thoughts that can bounce around in it like a beach ball at a concert. This process also creates an inner stillness that allows the mind, body, and spirit to relax and recharge. Some meditators find it helpful, especially initially, to focus on something specific, like their breath, a word, an object, a movement, or a sound. This pointed attention can aid in meditation, and create a deep sense of interior alignment and peace.

## What Does Meditation Do for You?

If you are like many people who are considering meditation, you want to know what it does for you, why you should incorporate it into your lifestyle, and how much you need to do to get the desired results. Science has begun to discover what yogis have known for thousands of years: Meditation promotes a sense of well-being and decreases negativity. Studies have demonstrated that meditation strengthens the left hemisphere of the brain, which controls the emotional response to stimuli (the level of reactivity). The brain's left hemisphere is also correlated with happiness and positivity. In other words, when you develop this part of your brain, your

perspective on life becomes more positive. It's like strengthening a muscle by regularly lifting weights.

Scientific findings clearly support the importance of a daily meditation practice. Investigators at Harvard Medical School, Massachusetts General Hospital, and Boston University concluded that meditation helps regulate the emotion-provoking center of the brain.[3] The researchers found that after practicing meditation for eight weeks, participants experienced a decrease in emotional response to negative stimuli. This decreased response was observed in brain scans as well as in participants' self-assessments of their own depression and anxiety. This study shows that meditation not only affects your mental state, it changes the actual structure of your brain. Michael J. Baime, M.D., researcher and clinician for the Penn Program for Stress Management, documented a connection between meditation and increased focus and clarity.[4] These skills are much needed in today's world, where innumerable stimuli are constantly and simultaneously vying for your attention. Meditation is a solution to the perpetual internal and external chatter.

Studies have also shown a correlation between meditation and health benefits. The research demonstrates that meditation has a favorable impact on a wide range of health issues, including anxiety, depression, ADHD (attention deficit/hyperactivity disorder), weight issues, asthma, high cholesterol, and heart attacks.[5] Evidence decidedly supports the positive effects of meditation. So, how much should you do?

## Developing a Meditation Practice

Time is precious, with the ever-increasing demands being placed on us. Therefore, when I am going to participate in something on a regular basis, I want to know how much time I need to spend in order to be effective. What is the least amount of effort that will yield the desired results? When I go to the gym, for example, I want to be in and out. I want to make the most of every moment, so I am achieving optimal results but not wasting time. I don't want to spend 20 minutes doing sit-ups if 15 will suffice. Conversely, I don't want to do 5 minutes of sit-ups if 12 will give me optimal results. According to an article in *Psychology Today*, research shows that as little as 10 minutes a day of meditation can create noticeable benefits, including reduced anxiety, decreased depression, and increased focus and clarity.[6] I think 10 minutes is doable even for those who profess extreme time constraints (which could include everyone at this point!).

Meditation has been around for thousands upon thousands of years and has been utilized by most cultures. Its many forms include breathing exercises, prayer, chanting, counting beads, and repeating mantras, to name just a few. The primary purpose of these practices is to find a place of stillness and to connect to something greater than oneself (within the framework of one's religion or culture).

Let's look at ways to incorporate ten minutes of meditation into your day. You can utilize any of a vast number of techniques to obtain beneficial results. I suggest choosing a method that you can envision implementing and that fits into your life. Unfortunately, if

you can't visualize doing it, it probably won't happen. Once you become comfortable incorporating some form of meditation into your daily routine, start to explore other techniques. Decide what works best for your individual needs. Maybe on certain days you will use one form, and on other days you will use a different one. That's great! Develop a meditation program that suits your style. There are days when I thoroughly enjoy sitting on a rock in my backyard, focusing on the sound of the birds chirping in harmony. Other days, I run like the wind (just kidding—my kids tell me I run like a turtle), focusing on my breathing and repeating a mantra in my head. (I'm sure my children are thankful that I don't run around town saying the mantra out loud.) There are yet other days when I am exhausted and enjoy lying down, visualizing light moving through my body as I breathe in rhythm with it.

One of my most powerful experiences with meditation occurred after a fabulous yoga class on the beach during a heat wave on Cape Cod. We had done yoga for over an hour, and beads of sweat were running down my arms. Nancy Curran, my mentor and yoga teacher, suggested that we go into the water and float on our backs in a technique she coined "Sea-vasana" (a play on *Savasana*, the yoga pose that invites a meditative state). As I lay drifting on the ocean currents, I experienced an amazing connection to nature, spirit, and ultimate bliss. It was a moment I will never forget, and I am thankful to have experienced it. I was *open* to the experience, which not only allowed me to gain an appreciation for a new and profound way of meditating but also gave me a new technique for my meditation toolbox.

Being open to trying new things in life gives us richer, deeper, and more meaningful experiences. Open yourself to forms of meditation that resonate with you. Each time you do, you will find out what works and what doesn't. Again, you might collect a number of meditation techniques and use different ones depending on your circumstances or your state of mind. Being stuck in an airplane seat for a few hours, for example, might be the perfect time to meditate. The technique you select for such a setting might be different than one you would choose to move from a state of agitation to calmness. Listen to the messages of your mind, body, and spirit to build your meditation practice. You will come to recognize which techniques belong in your meditation toolbox, and which one to pull out in any given situation.

## Meditation Tools and Techniques

One stereotype of meditation is that it is done while sitting cross-legged, torso stretched tall, arms resting on the knees, and eyes closed. My girls went through a period when they would make a game of pretending to meditate in the car. Hearing "Om-ing" sounds coming from the backseat, I would turn around to find them with legs crossed, eyes closed, hands resting on knees, and fingers in a circle position. Their playfulness made us all giggle but also gave me insight into the way many people view meditation. In one of my yoga classes, I remember being relieved to find out that you don't have to sit to meditate; if lying down is better for your body, go for it. That was such a relief for me. As a runner, I like to lie down with my feet up a wall to relieve the

pressure on my lower back. I am telling you this so you understand there really is no "right way" to meditate. Find what works best for you and will allow you to enjoy meditation's beneficial impact on your life.

*Deep Breathing*

One technique I often go to when the beach ball starts bouncing around in my head (that is, I am experiencing mental chaos) is simply focusing on my breathing. Your breathing can be a telltale sign of your mental state at any point in your day. Notice how you are breathing at breakfast, after you have cooled down from a workout, when you are engaged in an activity that brings you joy, and when you are feeling stress. Compare your breathing when you are anxious to after you have taken a bath or spent time gazing at the stars. Your breathing is probably different in these various scenarios.

According to Eastern yogic tradition, the body's vitality is dependent on the breath. Similarly, Western medicine has scientifically proven that deep breathing has a dramatic effect on the sympathetic and parasympathetic nervous systems. Shallow breathing is usually experienced when the sympathetic nervous system is stimulated—that is, when the body is in an elevated state of stress sometimes referred to as the fight-or-flight response, which I have mentioned elsewhere in this book. Due to the fast pace of daily living, multiple pressures, multitasking, poor eating habits, and the grip of technology, many people remain in this elevated state of stress for longer periods than the human body was designed for—which produces dis-ease, fatigue, depression, weight gain, and other maladies. Deep breathing can disrupt this heightened sense of alert and activate the parasympathetic nervous system, returning the body to a balanced and relaxed state.

Now, take a deep breath. How did that make you feel? Deep breathing can bring you a sense of calm. Just imagine if you were able to sustain that feeling for an extended period as a result of your consistent meditation practice. Now, take several deep breaths. For each breath, start by slowly inhaling and filling your lungs to full capacity. Did you even know your lungs could expand that far? When you think you are at full capacity, take in a little bit more air. Pause at the top of this breath. Then, slowly and mindfully, exhale until you think there is no air left in you. Then try to exhale just a little bit more. Pause before you begin to slowly inhale and expand your lungs to their full capacity again. Repeat this simple process. This is deep breathing. Taking a few moments each day to breathe consciously lays the foundation for your meditation practice. You can do it anywhere, anytime—sitting at your desk, relaxing in a peaceful spot, or lying in bed before falling sleep. The key is to be fully present and to pay attention to your breath.

At first, incorporate two five-minute sessions of mindful breathing into your day. Gradually increase the amount of time you spend in a single session. Note how your body and mind feel right after each session—and how your whole life changes for the better. Immediate results can include clarity, peace, and increased energy. Whole-life benefits are unique for each individual. Do you have better overall concentration, has your sleep quality improved, or are you feeling a general sense of contentment? These are only a few ways in which meditation can have a beneficial impact on your overall well-being.

*Sounds of Nature*

Whether you are a new meditator or a seasoned guru, there are days when stillness does not come easily. At these times, I find it both helpful and relaxing to connect with nature. It is ironic that on days when I *most* need to meditate, I feel less inclined to sit still for a while because my mind is racing, my to-do list is taunting me, and my stress level is high. It may seem counterintuitive to take a few minutes to slow down when you have so much to do, but it is in these moments that you become centered and recharge your batteries, producing clarity and optimal productivity. When my thoughts are frenetic, I find it constructive to go outside and listen to the birds. Focusing on the chirping of the different birds soothes me and moves me from my agitated state. These few moments in nature help ground me, giving me the lucidity to formulate solutions to the tasks or problems that had *brought* me to my agitated state. Intently concentrating on something is a form of meditation. Focusing on some form of nature—birds chirping, waves crashing, or trees rustling in a soft breeze—can restore your equilibrium and equanimity.

*Moving Meditation*

There are many forms of moving meditation, including yoga, tai chi, labyrinth walking, and running. Athletes from all sports talk about being "in the zone"— when they are so focused on the task at hand that they are capable of tuning everything else out. The best athletes in the world are the ones who have the most focus. You hear that golf is a mental game and that with many sports you need to "become one with the ball."

Similarly, intent focus during movement can help you enter the "meditation zone." I am a big fan of moving meditation. I enjoy the feeling of bliss following a heated yoga class, the clarity after walking a labyrinth, and the invigoration of a mindful run. I use these techniques from my meditation toolbox on a regular basis. The key to moving meditation is focus. That means turning off your portable MP3 player and being fully present. Concentrating on each step or breath will help you experience the utter contentment of a moving meditation. If you become distracted, take a deep breath and begin to focus once again on your movement in the moment.

*Mantra Meditation*

A mantra is a word or phrase that is consciously repeated over and over. It gives your brain something to focus on instead of the bouncing beach ball. Certain ancient sounds are considered sacred and are used to help transform one's life. "Om" is a mantra and a sacred Sanskrit sound that translates to a divine connection to a greater power; it both represents and transcends the past, present, and future. Although "Om" resonates for me during a yoga class or sitting on the floor of my bedroom, the ancient mantras are not as effective during my runs. When I run, I select a mantra that reflects the state of mind or being that I am hoping to achieve. This kind of mantra is similar to an affirmation in that it speaks to me both consciously and unconsciously. It is a declaration to me and to my higher power of what I hope to be or to create.

If I am having a particularly stressful day, I might repeat to myself "I am love" or "I am light." These

repeated words become repetitive thoughts, which help move me out of my distressed condition. Glimpsing a stress-less state like love or light assists me in recalibrating my thought patterns for the rest of the day. If a stressful situation arises later, I will sometimes find myself repeating my mantra; out of habit, it kicks in unconsciously when I feel anxiety. Therefore, I gain insight into my current mental state and decide whether I need to meditate. Sometimes, just recognizing the stressor that triggered the mantra helps bring me back to a centered state. Mantras can be incorporated effectively into many meditative activities, whether moving or still. This meditation tool can help bring calm and balance to your mind and create a lasting sense of well-being.

*Personalized Practice*

Meditation is very personal. What works for you may not be ideal for someone else. The key is to find a practice that speaks to you; helps you hear your inner guidance; and navigates you toward peace, harmony, and joy. There are all kinds of *pranayama* (Sanskrit for "controlled breathing") techniques that can give you the physiological response of relaxation and the psychological response of serenity. You may be able to achieve the same results from chanting, singing, dancing, painting, or gardening. The list is endless! What matters is that you engage in something you love that stills your mind and brings you into the present moment—instead of thinking about regrets from the past or concerns about the future. As I have said before, there is no "right way" to meditate. Do what works best for you and commit to making it a habit.

Meditation is one way to achieve inner calm when you feel frazzled by life. The techniques described above are a small sampling of the wide variety you can try. Hopefully, learning about the positive effects of meditation on your mind, body, and spirit will motivate you to begin, renew, or ramp up your own practice.

## Harmony in Action

For the next seven days, do the following:

1. Purposefully challenge yourself to put your technological devices away.

2. Notice when your breathing becomes shallow.

3. Take five minutes twice a day to quiet your mind through deep breathing.

Finding calm and inner harmony is essential to leading an inspired life. These states can be difficult to achieve, however, given the increasingly rapid pace of today's world. Finding ways to detach from the chaos of daily living will help ground you and facilitate the peace you wish to attain. Becoming aware of the role technology plays in your life will help you loosen its sometimes suffocating grip on you. Disengaging from technology will allow you to take a much-needed deep breath. Speaking of which, begin to incorporate deep breathing into your routine to help shut down the stress response that is constantly activated in your body. Play with the

tools and techniques of meditation until you develop your own individualized practice. As a final word about meditation and as a lead-in to the next pillar of the Home in Harmony Lifestyle, it is sometimes necessary to get quiet and go within in order to find answers to the fundamental questions that tug at your consciousness. When you incorporate meditation into your life, illuminating information emerges. In the grounded stillness that meditation provides, you are able to tap into profound answers about your passions and your purpose.

*Chapter Five*

# The Fourth Pillar: Your Inner Light

The fourth pillar of the Home in Harmony Lifestyle is inner light. We all know people who emanate positive energy. Typically, you want to be around them, because they are vibrant and uplifting. The idea of inner light makes me think of the New England–based clothing and accessories company Life is good. Their mascot, Jake, is a smiling stick figure who radiates good vibes. We have a Frisbee with Jake and the sentiment "Life is good" on it hanging in our garage. It is a reminder for all who enter to shine their light, be positive, and spread love and joy. The Frisbee was a Father's Day gift for my husband, who does all of these things.

This chapter will help you discover what brings you true satisfaction and joy. Many people in Western

society are so busy acquiring things and "keeping up with the Joneses" that they have lost touch with what really makes them happy. They are no longer able to see what truly fulfills them. If this is true for you, we will peel back the layers so you can get in touch with your essence—lifting the veil on your inner light.

### Where Is Your Joy?

We all experience negative feelings from time to time. How we maneuver through these moments determines our ability to lead vibrant, joy-filled, and abundant lives. Feeling true joy keeps a person's emotional state from oscillating wildly with the currents of uncertainty, disappointment, and fear. Realizing that joy, rather than money or possessions, feeds the soul will help you connect to your inner light. Though joy may seem elusive to you now, it becomes attainable when you get in touch with your own desires and passions—and stop trying to meet the expectations of yourself and others.

## What Is Joy?

True joy is felt in one's core. In our culture, there is confusion between feeling happy for a moment and finding inner contentment regardless of the situation. The latter is a permanent state of being, whereas the former is a state that comes and goes. Temporary happiness is dependent on what is happening in the moment. For example, you might receive a compliment that gives you a sense of contentment, but moments later, another remark leaves you sad or uncomfortable. Think about a few questions: When a situation doesn't go your way, are you able to regain your equilibrium because you know, deep down, this disappointment is only temporary—or are you thrown off balance? Do you feel delighted as you purchase a coveted new item, only for that sensation to dissipate a few hours later, leaving you wanting something else? If you rely on an outside source—a compliment, a work success, a new purchase—for happiness, the feeling is only temporary. Your bliss will vanish as soon as something goes awry, or sooner. The goal is to move from a temporary experience of happiness to permanent joy.

Studies have shown that children laugh 300 to 400 times a day but adults, on average, only 15. Over time, responsibilities and the ability to reason take over, and a state of serious-mindedness sets in. We become disengaged from the innate mechanism that registers joy, because we are so focused on checking off our to-dos and satisfying our wants. Laughter is one indicator of your sense of fulfillment. It is critical to bring back your laughter, by finding your joy.

## Looking Inside

Let's look at how to bring your laughter—and your joy—back. I am reminded of a children's story that was a favorite in our home as the kids were growing up, "The Jester Has Lost His Jingle," by David Saltzman. The story conveys a profound message for young and old—and based on the statistics about laughter, maybe more adults should read it. It explains how the Jester is banished by the King one day for not being funny; in fact, laughter

is missing throughout the kingdom. As the Jester heads out into the big world, he is determined to find happiness and bring it back to the kingdom—the classic "hero's journey." On his adventures, he comes to realize that happiness is not something he can bring back from the outside world; rather, it is held within the kingdom. The metaphor, of course, is that joy comes from within, not from without.

"The Jester Has Lost His Jingle" illustrates two very important concepts about joy. The first is that looking outside ourselves for joy will make it elusive. The second is that to find joy, we must look inside. In this chapter, we will examine ways to find your inner joy—and to remain in a joyful state permanently. The path to experiencing your innate, deep-seated bliss is discovering your passion and purpose and sharing them with the world—thus radiating your inner light.

## What Brings You Joy?

Love and joy are closely related. When you do what you love, it brings you joy. Have you ever noticed that when you are doing something you love, time flies? Often in these moments of intense focus, you lose track of time. Begin to observe which activities have this effect on you, and then incorporate more of them into your daily life. Joy is our *natural state*. The pressures of the typical lifestyle, however, can cause us to become unbalanced and out of touch with our innate joy. Joy can feel not only inaccessible but unattainable. The first step in finding permanent joy is noticing which moments or activities in your day make you laugh or fill you with

enthusiasm. These moments, when experienced consistently, will bring back your "jingle."

Exploring what truly gives you joy might be a foreign concept to you. As a society, we have been taught that fulfillment comes from external sources. Our culture has convinced us that acquiring things or becoming what the world views as successful will make us happy. However, the ladder of external success is infinite; that is, we can never reach the top because we will never be permanently satisfied with what we have achieved. The ladder is also a slippery slope; our failures in the world's eyes can send us plummeting down the rungs. When you begin to cultivate joy *within*, you are able to experience unwavering peace in the successful moments *and* in the tumultuous times.

Society's expectations and cultural beliefs have a strong influence on how we live. It is time to wake up and live *on your own terms*. Arianna Huffington put it well in her commencement address at Smith College in May 2013: "Don't buy society's definition of success. Because it's not working for anyone. It's not working for women, it's not working for men, it's not working for polar bears, it's not working for the cicadas that are apparently about to emerge and swarm us. It's only truly working for those who make pharmaceuticals for stress, diabetes, heart disease, sleeplessness, and high blood pressure."[1] It is time to shed the constraints of what others would like your life to be.

People often get so caught up in the seemingly never-ending responsibilities of daily life that they don't take time for themselves. If you are feeling frazzled by existence, how do you find the time to incorporate uplifting activities into your day? Just as when you don't have time

to meditate *but need to most*, it is critical to participate in inspiring activities even when life seems overwhelming. Taking time to fill your spirit grounds and centers you so you can be more productive, stay open to opportunities, and move through turbulent times with ease and grace. Isn't it worth figuring out what brings you joy and incorporating it into your routine?

So, what makes your heart sing? When do you feel contentment? What activities cause you to lose track of time—gardening, playing hockey, decorating? Because we are all unique individuals, what makes *you* happy is going to be different from what brings someone else joy. Get in touch with what works for *you*. Of course, you may enjoy a number of things. I love to do yoga; paint; and sit on the beach, smelling the ocean air. When we moved from Connecticut to Massachusetts, we picked a spot that was close to the water because of its rejuvenating effect on me. I purposefully try to connect with the ocean air at least once a day, even if that means a quick drive by the water. Start to notice what recharges your proverbial batteries. Is it sipping a cup of tea in your quiet kitchen before the kids get home? Blasting your favorite music and dancing around the living room? Take some time today and in the coming week to notice what brings you joy.

## What Brought You Joy as a Child?

If you are beginning to squirm in your seat because you have no idea what fulfills you, let's look at some ways to ease your discomfort and set you on your path to joy. If you tend to equate happiness with some of the

examples given earlier—newly acquired items or acco-
lades at work—let's explore a new perspective. As demonstrated earlier, children are much more in touch with
unbridled joy than adults are. Think back to your own
childhood. What things did you love to do? I'm not talking about the structured activities your parents signed
you up for—unless you truly enjoyed them. If I were
to ask one of my daughters this question 20 years from
now, she would say that hockey was her sacred activity.
She feels an intense passion around this sport, which
she has played since she was three. She can't fit enough
hockey into her day. (She was mad at my husband and
me last year because we wouldn't let her play for more
than three teams.)

But our childhood pleasures aren't always so obvi-
ous. When I was a teenager, my mother, brother, and I
moved to a new home after my parents divorced. I was
excited to decorate my room and create a space I could
call my own. The house was a contemporary Cape that
my mom still lives in today. Over the front door was a
large, round, modern pendant light. My mother couldn't
stand the piece, and it was the first thing she removed,
replacing it with a classic brass fixture. As the pendant
light came down, I asked my mom if we could hang it
in my room. I also asked if we could put it on a dimmer
so it would glow like the moon at night. I then installed
a wicker hanging chair by my window, so I could swing
for hours while talking to my friends on the phone
under the soft glow of my "moon." In other words, my
passion for design started at a young age. I am thankful
that I have been able to incorporate that early joy into
my adult experience. A friend of mine mentioned she

would play imaginary school when she was a little girl; now she is a teacher.

Reflect on the activities you were drawn to as a child. This perspective can help you find fulfillment now.

## A Year of Doing What You Love

If looking back at your childhood leaves you questioning your ability to connect to things that recharge and invigorate you, let's take a different approach. This exercise might open you up to more possibilities for restoring your natural state of joy. When I have clients who are really stuck, I often ask them a simple question. Contemplating this question can give you a new perspective on how you are living your life and if small changes—or major shifts—need to be made. Hopefully, it will shed light on how you can begin to glow.

Here is the question: If a source gave you unlimited funds, with the only stipulations being that you had to spend the money within a year and you had to do something you loved, what would that be? Note that the money would *enable* you to do what you loved, whether it helped you pay your bills during the year or covered the cost of the activity. Take some time to really evaluate this question. What would your year be like? What would you be doing, and where? One day in my own exuberantly fulfilling year might include an afternoon looking at the beautiful ocean while writing books to help people live to their fullest potential, after a morning spent paddle-boarding with my husband and meditating on the beach. In the evening, I would luxuriate in the presence of my children as we ate a healthy dinner under the moon and stars in a tropical paradise. On another day, I might spend time working with color, either designing or painting.

As you can see, pondering this question helps you recognize what fills your spirit. There is no right or wrong answer, and your picture can evolve. When designing your inspired year, remember that it revolves around *you* and *your* needs—not the expectations you have for yourself or the ones others impose on you. We get enough of that in real life! For this exercise, let go of the "shoulds" and "have-tos," which drain your energy. Take this opportunity to plan the ideal year in your life—a year filled with things that make you happy. I am excited to hear about your vision!

Hopefully, you have begun to discover what truly brings you joy. Incorporating these elements into your daily life helps recharge your spirit, which is necessary for radiating good vibes and achieving permanent joy. Taking time to rejuvenate yourself keeps you centered and enables you to navigate both positive and negative times with ease. From your foundation of joy, you can shine your light, spreading love and happiness in the world.

## *The Habit of Happiness*

We are products of our habits. Habits make up 75 to 90 percent of our behavior each day.[2] As we have discussed, becoming aware of your habits and making a conscious effort to replace the negative ones with positive ones is key to leading your best life. In the previous

section, you began to identify what brings you joy. Incorporating habits of happiness into your routine is the next step in living with passion and purpose. But how do you add activities to a day that is already filled with commitments? Start small. Take one purposeful baby step at a time. Build momentum. Utilize the principles of habit formation to introduce a fulfilling new behavioral pattern into your life. Experiencing inspirational moments will help you move through your day with grace. You will think, speak, and act from a place of contented connection.

I find the practice of yoga to be joyful, inspiring, and centering. It touches my soul more than any other activity. I prefer heated, flowing yoga that allows me to move gracefully as if in a trance as I sweat out puddles of toxins. While doing yoga, I sometimes experience moments when I am truly one with my body and breath; at these times, I can feel the tingling of my spirit connecting with the universal Source of all that is. After such an uplifting experience, I am able to walk through my day in a bliss-filled state. Chaos seems to evaporate in the presence of my serenity.

You might think I would be racing to repeat any experience that created such a euphoric high. On the contrary, I don't usually think about how I will feel after class when I am getting ready on the morning of a "yoga day." Putting on my yoga clothes, without thought, gives me no excuse *not* to go. If I were to think about it, I would focus on the grueling hour and a half of push-ups, plank position, and boat pose that leaves my muscles screaming, "No more!" Instead, I have a set schedule; I know I am going to the yoga studio, and I

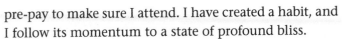

pre-pay to make sure I attend. I have created a habit, and I follow its momentum to a state of profound bliss.

Identify an inspiring behavior that you would like to include in your day. Arrange for the time, space, and other circumstances necessary. If it is helpful, take out a calendar and block off time for the activity. I have created room in my life for yoga and established the habit to ensure its execution.

## Create Lasting Positive Habits

Now that you have found what feeds your soul and have prepared a spot for it in your life, you must make a serious commitment to yourself to keep doing it for four weeks. Making a commitment to yourself is not something to take lightly. When you break a promise to yourself, two things occur. First, you are angry with yourself for not following through and achieving what you had set out to do. (This is why baby steps will move mountains.) Your anger is compounded by disappointment in yourself, which leads to a feeling of unworthiness and then insecurity. You may think things like, "I'm no good at it anyway," "I never can . . . ," and "I don't have the willpower." These self-sabotaging statements lower your self-worth and drain your vitality. So make sure you commitment is realistic.

For example, if you want spend time gardening but haven't done it in years, you might start with caring for containers of healthy herbs or vibrantly colored flowers. The last thing you want to do is give yourself an unachievable task, like planting an entire garden in a day. Decide that every Friday (or whatever day is best for

you) at a specific time (again, whatever works best in your schedule) you are going to do what it is you love. If you hope to eventually grow a garden, break the project into tasks you can do during those first four weeks of habit formation. By making the tasks achievable, no matter what your spirit-filling activity is—gardening, singing, dancing, playing tennis—there is a double positive effect. You are doing something that makes your soul sing *and* you feel good for keeping a promise to yourself.

After accomplishing each baby step, celebrate your success! By acknowledging and honoring your progress, you are more likely to stick with the activity, thereby creating a lasting positive habit. You might gift yourself a bouquet of beautiful flowers or treat yourself to a massage. Recognizing the sacred moments in the process of incorporating something joyful into your life is a win-win celebration of your spirit!

## Habitual Drains

As you know by now, habits control a large portion of our lives. Studies show that replacing bad habits with good ones is much more effective than trying to eliminate the habitual behavior altogether. Begin to evaluate which of your habits are draining your energy. Then you can swap these out for new habits that offer positive outcomes.

There are activities we engage in that not only deplete our essence but consume our time. For instance, most people struggle to find a balance with technology. If you are rolling your eyes because you don't want to hear it, it's time to look at your relationship to technology. Even if you are not rolling your eyes, you should examine the role of technology in your life. In the morning, I purposefully walk by my office without entering it because I know that if I move toward my computer, I will be lured by its influence. I can easily become distracted by the e-mails vying for attention in my clogged inbox. I know that I am better served by first participating in one of my regular centering activities, like running, yoga, or meditation. This habit brings me into balance and helps me link to serenity and joy. I can then effectively process my electronic messages from a position of inner harmony, a state that engenders perspective, clarity, and focus. I sidestep the fear, anxiety, and frustration often associated with responding to the needs and requests of others. It is critical not only to unplug from technology throughout your day but to begin your day with a habit that connects you to joy and activates your inner guidance. Inner guidance is the whispering of your spirit or soul. To hear this counsel, you must get quiet and listen. It will steer you toward positive experiences in your life, in a cycle that perpetuates joy.

Because we are all unique, what drains me doesn't necessarily have the same effect on you. Let go of your own expectations and those of others. Only *you* know what depletes you or energizes you. Begin to listen actively to your inner guidance. This internal navigation system will help you find your joy. When I was young, I wasn't sure what I wanted to be when I grew up. A high value was placed on education by my family (and by society), so I was expected to go to college. Fortunately, I was ecstatic about the opportunity. Entering Boston College, I was amazed at all the people who already knew what they wanted to major in or even what they wanted to

do when they finished school. I felt a little lost. My family thought I should go into education because, in their experience, most women were either nurses or teachers and then they settled down and had a family. At my core, I knew teaching wasn't my calling. Initially, however, I acquiesced to the expectations of others, mostly because I wasn't sure what I wanted to do. Thankfully, on some level, I listened to the stirrings of my soul and took classes in human development and psychology.

But that first year, I struggled through classes on elementary education. Was this what it meant to grow up? Were you stuck doing something forever that didn't make your soul sing? I thought, "I really should do this to make my family proud." But I realized education was not my true calling in the course of a week as a substitute teacher at an inner-city school. A third grader in my class climbed out the bathroom window and walked to the convenience store down the street. (I learned later that this was typical behavior for this child.) A middle schooler also threw a metal chair at me. In each instance, my heart was heavy that these children were hurting so much. To me, their actions were evidence of internal pain, and they were acting out in the hope that an outsider might help them. In those moments, my heart told me my path was to help heal the many who were suffering. Indeed, taking this path ignited my passion and empowered me. Teaching was not my calling. (With that said, I am filled with immense gratitude for all the patient and gifted teachers who bless us with their service every day.) Listening to my inner guidance moved me from a situation that was draining my energy to my true purpose.

We have explored several steps in creating an internal foundation of joy. First, connect to what makes you laugh, lights your fire, and brings you happiness. Next, examine your habits to determine whether they are life-giving or draining. Finally, replace negative habits with uplifting ones.

## Shine Your Light

We have discussed how feeling joy is natural and how incorporating joyful activities into your life will encourage your inherent joy. Again and again, studies have shown a connection between *sharing your gifts* and feeling true joy. It's as if a higher power wants us to find our gifts and share them with the world.

At some point, most of us ask the fundamental questions about life. Some might wonder, "Who am I?" or "Why am I here?" Others might desire to know, "What is the purpose of life?" or "What is the meaning of my life?" These inquiries are part of the natural process of wanting to find a deeper significance to existence. At their core is the innate need to live a purpose-centered life. Existential questions play a role in the evolutionary process of "up-leveling." By up-leveling, I mean moving toward the next goal, wish, or desire. We are designed, individually and as a species, to continuously grow and experience the next stage of our being. Some might call this finding our spiritual essence. Becoming conscious of this innate drive is key to designing an inspired life.

As you move beyond being satisfied with negative habitual patterns and you consciously incorporate joy-filled moments into your life, your inner light will begin

to shine. When your inner radiance breaks through the dense fog of unconscious living, you will become a magnet for positive situations and people. You will give off a favorable energy that others want to be a part of—instead of a draining energy that people would rather avoid. We have all been around individuals who tend to deplete us. These people are sometimes referred to as "energy vampires." Unfortunately, interacting with these individuals can be as noxious as encountering chemical toxins. It is important to decide whether you will include energy vampires in your life. Sometimes, it is unavoidable. The first step is to recognize that someone *is* an energy vampire. Then you must assess whether or not you are really willing to put up with this person's draining behavior for the sake of the relationship or connection. Finally, it is important to put boundaries in place to minimize the energy vampire's depleting effect on you. That being said, you ultimately want to radiate good vibes so that you attract people and experiences that are positive and life-enhancing. One way to do this is to share your gifts with the world.

## Sharing Your Gifts

I am always amazed at people who have unique talents. My three girls and I have a weekly ritual: We curl up and watch *American Idol* together. When hockey, homework, and speaking schedules permit, we gather as enthusiastic fans. Sometimes we hold up homemade signs for our favorite artists or engage in discussions about why some contestants are liked and others might be having an off week. I am filled with gratitude as these incredibly talented souls share their gifts with the world. In those moments when I get goosebumps on my arms, I know I am hearing their core essence. By bravely shining their light, these singers inspire all who witness them.

I am struck that we *all* have incredible gifts. These endowments of love and light are meant to be shared with the world. Our gifts vary, of course. One person might be good at making dinner for a friend in need, while another does backflips in the Olympics. Regardless of the particular talent, each gift is sacred. It adds to the greater good through a ripple effect that flows from one person to the next. Each contribution is a divine expression of core essence; therefore, each gift is extraordinary, no matter what it is.

You might find that you have more than one gift to share. As an interior designer, I shared my gifts of design and color. Then I realized I could incorporate all of my passions into a single offering, the Home in Harmony Lifestyle. Once I made this transition, positive situations presented themselves, and I drew people into my life who could help me share my gifts. There is a force, whatever you choose to call it, that wants us to discover our gifts and supports us in our efforts to share them with the world.

## Affirmative Action Steps

To recap from the previous sections, a critical step in finding your inner glow is examining your habitual patterns. Walking around in an unconscious fog disengages you from the present moment and distracts you from realizing your potential. Break down your day

and determine which moments are life-enhancing and which are energy-depleting; replace your negative habits or remove them from your life. Also, identify which occasions *fill* your spirit. During these moments, it is important to be fully present. Create *more* of these experiences, to enhance your well-being; this is a form of self-care. The skill of nurturing yourself is one worth developing. It allows you to connect to your inner guidance, feel the support of the Divine, and live vibrantly in the moment.

Once you have truly assessed where you are, look at *where you want to be*. We have talked at length about finding what brings you joy. Another way to discover your purpose and passion is to determine what your ideal life would look like and feel like. Notice what is currently happening in your life and then ponder what you *want* to be happening. Imagine if those American Idol contestants never contemplated the possibility of singing beyond the shower. Where would they be right now? Shifting your attention to the ideal helps bring your potential into focus. Then you can take action toward that potential, transforming it from possible to probable. In every area of your life, begin to ask yourself, "Is this my ideal vision?" or "What would be my ideal vision?" Blinders are placed on horses to keep them from being distracted by their peripheral view. In a similar way, focusing on the ideal helps you clearly see what you hope to create, informing you how to design your inspired life.

Your journey will likely have turns and detours. These deviations from the path will help you experience a wide variety of life's offerings, allowing you to hone in on the ones you enjoy most. Indeed, these episodes make up the splendid and unique tapestry of your life. There are times, however, when your unconscious thoughts and beliefs may hold you back from realizing your joy. Become conscious of these habitual patterns, which keep you living in a fog (as opposed to enjoying the crystal-clear vision of inspired living). Notice the thoughts that replay in your mind. Repetitive thoughts commonly relate to self-worth, money, ability, and appearance: "I can't do that." "I'm not good enough." "I'm so fat." "If people knew the real me, they wouldn't like me." "Money doesn't grow on trees." Shift these negative thoughts to positive ones: "I am lovable." "I am light." "I am worthy to have good things happen in my life." "I am deserving of abundance."

Negative thoughts are often residual messages heard from caregivers, siblings, teachers, or coaches during the formative years. It is critical to assess what these messages are and where they came from in order to release their grip on your mind. Imagine transforming your dozens of negative habitual thoughts into positive ones. What a burden would be lifted from your shoulders! The heavy cloak that shields you from feeling deep joy would fall away.

Again, the first step in actualizing your ideal life is determining what that means to you. Next, you must identify the unseen and unconscious obstacles, such as habitual patterns, that are blocking you from fulfilling your purpose. Bringing clarity to these two areas gives you the vision, focus, and awareness needed to realize your inspired life. Your internal navigation system will assist you every step of the way, from finding your purpose and passion to achieving your ideal existence. Meditation can help you connect to your soul, to receive

its guidance. You will never regret the effort involved in finding your divine gifts, which bring you joy and support you in radiating good vibes.

## Harmony in Action

For the next seven days, do the following:

1.  Write about all the current or past activities that bring or have brought you joy.

2.  Write down the expectations that you have for yourself or that others have for you.

3.  Write a description of your ideal year.

Identifying what fills your spirit and brings you exuberant joy is the first step in lifting the veil on your inner light, the fourth and final pillar of the Home in Harmony Lifestyle. Envisioning your ideal life helps you take action toward it. Habitual thoughts, words, and actions have the potential to hold you back, but you can shift negative habits to uplifting practices that support you on your journey. This work helps strengthen your inner foundation of serenity and joy. From this solid base, you can courageously share your gifts with the world, shining your radiant light! In the following chapter, we will look more concretely at how to achieve this extraordinary but completely realistic goal.

*Chapter Six*

# Putting It All Together

I wish that someone had given me a blueprint for leading my best life years ago. I am thankful that I can share my more than 20 years of academic and experiential insights with you to help you design your own inspired life. Practicing the Home in Harmony Lifestyle will guide you to a healthy, vibrant, and joyful existence more quickly than my own meandering path led *me* to this destination! Although my life has had its share of trials, I am grateful for the journey—which has also been filled with glorious moments that have left me in awe. Each moment, good or bad, has brought me to where I am today. Collectively, these moments have given me the experience, training, and expertise to teach this amazing lifestyle to you. The information in this book is intended to help you define and navigate *your own* sacred path.

### Create a Vision Board

In previous chapters, I advised you to "start small" and take "baby steps." I do believe this is the most effective way to change behavior, incorporate fresh strategies, and adopt a new lifestyle. However, for a moment, let's work backward, starting from the end: your ideal life. Look at the big picture. What does this ideal life look like? Who is with you? What activities are you participating in? In recent years, vision boards have become more and more popular. This insightful device can help you explore and answer the above questions. For those who don't know, a vision board is a tool for manifesting your optimal life. It consists of any type of board displaying images or words that you have thoughtfully selected to represent your future. I recommend that you place the board where you can view it regularly. I have used vision boards and am awed by their power—which comes from taking time to focus on how you want your life to be. This clarity, coupled with the intention behind visualizing your ideal life, creates inspired momentum, fueled by grace. By clearly deciding what you want, and illustrating it in concrete form, you are sending a direct letter to the universe—your co-creator.

An added benefit of making a vision board is that it helps you "move out of the way" and let your subconscious guide you. You might utilize meditation to access your subconscious (your internal guidance system); that is, meditating can help you get in touch with where your spirit wants you to go. Examining your habits, which are subconscious patterns, is also important; habits can give you clues as to how your mind is operating beneath your conscious awareness. In addition, pay attention to your feelings, which are great indicators of what brings you joy. For example, if you are flipping through a magazine and see a picture that makes your heart sing, it might be appropriate to include it on your vision board.

To create your vision board, follow these steps:

1. Decide what you want to unfold in your life.

2. Become clear on how your ideal life looks and feels.

3. Use pictures to illustrate this vision.

4. Allow the pictures to remind you daily, on conscious and unconscious levels, of what you truly want.

Keep in mind that your vision board should reflect the big picture of your life.

### *Commit to Yourself*

Another important element in creating the life of your dreams is making a pledge to yourself to take appropriate action. The easiest way to carry out this commitment to yourself is to implement habitual behaviors that will lead you toward your envisioned life. Here are some examples:

- If you are hoping to create an inspired home, look at your calendar and determine times that work best for clutter-clearing.

- If you want to start a clean-eating lifestyle, make time to shop for healthy ingredients and to try new recipes.

- If you are hoping to experience calm in your life, promise yourself that you will practice meditation on a regular basis.

- If you are trying to connect to your inner joy, begin to notice and even write down what makes you smile.

In our hectic world, it is important to schedule an activity into your day or week so that you actually do it and *continue* to do it until it becomes a habit. Otherwise, it is too easy to forget about the activity or become too busy to make time for it. Entering commitments into your calendar gives them priority status, making the chances greater that you will follow through on them and ultimately form a desirable habit.

### Make a Plan

Now that you have become clear on your ideal life, it is important to put a plan in place to make your dreams come true. Break down the big picture of what you want to accomplish into easy, achievable steps. For instance, if you are hoping to have a clean-eating lifestyle within three months, divide that goal into manageable pieces. Map out small steps, or mini-goals, that will get you where you want to be—without feeling overwhelmed. Consider what you want to accomplish in the first and second months, and the weeks within those months, and the days within those weeks, in order to attain the final results in the third month.

Creating any meaningful change—especially implementing the Home in Harmony Lifestyle—is essentially a four-step process that can be signified by the acronym *HOME*:

1. **H**, for **habits:** Assess your life and the habits that define it.

2. **O**, for **objective:** Determine what it is you are hoping to create.

3. **M**, for **manageable steps:** Break down your actions toward your objective into achievable pieces.

4. **E**, for **energy:** Use your innate power, your inner vitality, to stick to these new behaviors until they become life-affirming habits.

Let's look at these four steps so that you are able to implement them easily. The first step is *assessing where you currently are*. What is working and what is not working in your life? Hopefully, you have gained an appreciation of how habits touch every part of your life. Becoming aware of your habitual thoughts and behaviors is a fundamental aspect of designing your optimal life.

The second step is *clearly defining what you want in your life*. This clarity will help you navigate toward your objective, or goal. Utilizing tools like the vision board we discussed earlier or engaging your inner guidance through meditation can help you focus on what you want.

The third step is *breaking your vision down into manageable and achievable steps*. Baby steps allow you to make changes at a pace that is not exhausting. You will build the momentum needed to arrive at the life of your dreams.

The fourth step is *implementing positive behaviors and sticking with them.* Doing away with habits that do not serve you and mindfully incorporating positive practices will move you from living unconsciously to attentively constructing a balanced, vital, and vibrant life. Penciling in time on your calendar is a simple trick for making positive thoughts and behaviors a priority. Then repeat, repeat, repeat! Reinforce habit formation by celebrating your successes. Carrying out the actions necessary to attain your ideal life should be a joyous experience of awareness, growth, and development.

### Actualize the Four Pillars

Now that you have become clear on your big vision, determined what behaviors you want to incorporate into your life, and identified the small steps needed to achieve your desired results, let's apply these ideas specifically to the four pillars of the Home in Harmony Lifestyle.

## Your Inspired Home

Look around your home and identify what you love about it. What aspects make it a sanctuary for your soul and a nest for your family? On the contrary, what areas make you cringe or roll your eyes because you don't like what you see or there are things you need to attend to? Do you notice any furnishings or products that are unhealthful or toxic? Can you incorporate items that are health-promoting instead? Keep in mind that it *is* possible to live in an environment in which you love every element, down to the smallest detail. You may find it helpful to walk around each room, writing down the positives and negatives in a notebook. Be honest with yourself, and determine what you truly like or don't like based on your current beliefs and values.

Sometimes we hold on to particular items out of habit. They served us at one time but no longer do so. Over the years, we grow, adapt, and change. For example, in your 20s, you might have loved vibrant yellow in your space; but now, in your 40s, you are better served by more grounding colors. In other words, it's time to paint the walls! Similarly, if you inherited a piece of furniture from a relative who doesn't hold a warm place in your heart, why make space in your haven for a reminder of this person? Honestly assessing your space will help you determine *where you are*, the first step in creating an inspired home—the first pillar of the Home in Harmony Lifestyle.

The next step is determining what you want *in* and *from* your inspired home. Imagine living in a healthy, nurturing, and beautiful environment. What does that mean to you? What images come to mind? When you visualize walking into your ideal living space, what do you see? How do you feel? What do you hear? How does it smell? Take some time to meditate on these aspects of your perfect home. Writing down your thoughts can help you become clear on the type of environment that will support you best. Clearly define the mood you wish to feel while in the space and the types of activities you hope to participate in there. Do you desire a soothing retreat that promotes quiet time—or an entertainer's dream home that encourages lively dinner parties? Notice other spaces that speak to you, whether they are photos in magazines, friends' homes, or hotels or

restaurants that you love. Collect images of these inspiring spaces, for your reference.

Once you have determined the grand vision for your home, start to take small actions toward realizing it. Use the tips and suggestions discussed earlier to make your home healthy; beautiful; and supportive of you physically, mentally, and spiritually. Create a plan, broken down into manageable steps, for what you hope to achieve in the upcoming year—for each month within the year, each week within each month, and each day within each week. A blueprint like this takes the guesswork—and stress—out of making progress toward your goal, especially if that ideal seems lofty to you. Breaking down your objective into actionable pieces will help you advance gracefully from where you are to where you want to be.

Positive habits will help you create, manage, and sustain your ideal home. Keep in mind that we are continuously evolving beings, and our living environments reflect this fact. Allow your space to develop, transform, and adapt with you. On a regular basis, assess which items in your home uplift you or deplete you. Make time in your schedule to clear clutter and maintain your home's organization. Celebrate your successes, no matter how small. With each little step, you move closer to creating your Home in Harmony Lifestyle.

## Your Healthy Body

The first step in creating a healthy body is determining your current level of physical vitality. Do you find yourself fatigued and lethargic at different points in your day? Do you consume the standard American diet, which is heavy in processed foods containing refined sugars, hydrogenated fats, and toxins? Do you typically bring home cleaning and beauty products made with noxious chemicals? The answers to questions like these will help you assess your lifestyle and habits, which have a huge impact on your wellness.

For this pillar of the Home in Harmony Lifestyle, clearly define what a healthy body means to you. For some, it might mean being free of toxic body burden; for others, it might involve shedding a few extra pounds. Visualize your long-term goal of vibrant health. Then break down that big picture into achievable steps. I recommend that you get your blood pumping by incorporating movement into your day; then take it to the next level and *sweat* out the toxins that have accumulated in your body. Actively choose whole and nourishing foods, healthful products, and activities that contribute to your vitality. If you have ingrained habits that are far from healthy, take action to replace them with nurturing routines and life-affirming patterns—and then stick with them.

## Your Calm Mind

In today's world, it is critical to maintain a calm mind, which is the third pillar of the Home in Harmony Lifestyle. Amidst the frenetic activity, pressures, commitments, and technological distractions of modern life, it is critical to assess where you are mentally and where you want to be. Sometimes, the merry-go-round of these influences is spinning so fast that it is hard to

get off. You need to figure out how to gain control of your life—and step *off* the merry-go-round, onto solid ground. Examining the habitual thoughts and behaviors that create stress in your life is the first step in achieving inner serenity.

Determine what inner calm, harmony, and peace mean to you. Pay attention to the experiences that help move you toward these states. I love sitting on the beach, listening to the waves crash as seagulls glide across the sky. This activity helps ground me and allows me to transcend the cacophony of the modern world. Break down the process of finding inner calm into manageable steps, utilizing the tools presented in chapter 4. Meditating, for example, is known to bring mental stillness as well as open the door to your inner guidance. Consider that you are more likely to repeat behaviors that resonate with you and that you enjoy. By incorporating your preferred techniques into your routine in a doable way, you will assimilate them into your lifestyle.

## Your Inner Light

The fourth pillar of the Home in Harmony Lifestyle involves finding your joy and letting your inner light shine! Answering the big questions in life can be challenging. "Who am I?" "Why am I here?" "What is my purpose?" Evaluating where you are in relation to these questions is an integral part of living passionately and on purpose. Essentially, what habitual thoughts and behaviors have held you back from the extraordinary expression of *you*?

Practicing the third pillar of the Home in Harmony Lifestyle—finding your inner connection to calm—makes achieving the fourth pillar much easier. Linking to the quiet knowing in your heart assists you in addressing many existential questions. This inner guidance helps guide you along your path and gives you the courage to live to your fullest potential. Once you become aware of the big picture of your purpose, plan to take baby steps in your effort to achieve it. Proceeding methodically and manageably toward lifting the veil on your inner light will give you the confidence to continue. The world *needs* your light, where there is darkness. It is time to access your inner joy so you can shine!

## *Your Home in Harmony Lifestyle*

The Home in Harmony Lifestyle is a template for extraordinary and inspired living. I encourage you to utilize its four pillars as the structure for a beautifully designed life. Having an inspired home, a healthy body, a calm mind, and a radiant inner light will help you not just survive but *thrive*. More specifically, you want to develop a home environment that nurtures you physically, mentally, and spiritually; a level of health and vitality that allows you to move through each day with grace and ease; a tranquil mind that rises above the chaos of modern living; and a state of passionate purpose that lets you share you shining gifts with the world.

To support you further in achieving these goals, I have provided supplemental information in the two appendices that follow. In Appendix A, you will find detailed lists of household toxins, pesticide-contaminated fruits and

vegetables to avoid, plants that can be used to improve indoor air quality, essential foods to have in your pantry, and recommended cleaning products and beauty supplies. In Appendix B, I offer menus for entertaining as well as healthy recipes for delicious dishes that include many of the nutrient-dense superfoods discussed in the book.

## Harmony in Action

In the next seven days, do the following:

1. Identify one small thing you can do to start creating your inspired home.

2. Think of a baby step you can take toward having a healthy body.

3. Implement one technique that resonates with you in creating a calm mind.

4. Incorporate one activity into your week that brings you unbridled joy.

As you know by now, implementation of the four pillars of the Home in Harmony Lifestyle requires the conscious replacement of negative habits with supportive ones. My hope is that you will assess where you are, determine where you want to be, and take the steps necessary to lead a healthy, joy-filled, and vibrant existence . . . your best life . . . your Home in Harmony Lifestyle.

# Appendix A

# Household Toxins and Healthy Home Choices

This appendix is designed to make the Home in Harmony Lifestyle as tangible and accessible to you as possible, so you can minimize the toxic items in your environment and incorporate healthful products that promote vibrant living. First, I will give you detailed information about household toxins, such as those found in cleaning products, personal care products, and furnishings—along with quick fixes for dealing with them. I will also tell you about pesticide-ridden fruits and vegetables that you should avoid. Then I will offer suggestions for plants you can bring into your home to purify the air. Finally, I will help take the guesswork out of shopping by providing lists of recommended cleaning products, personal care products, and groceries.

You can find continuously updated product lists, tips, and suggestions for vibrant living at www.christaoleary .com. These solutions will help you attain and maintain your Home in Harmony Lifestyle!

### Toxins in the Home

This section identifies and describes some of the most common household toxins. Then it offers information relating specifically to chemicals found in home furnishings, so you can design or adapt your living environment to be as nontoxic as possible. I will also provide several quick-reference tables of the toxic ingredients found in common household products, so you can be fully aware of what you are bringing into your home. Finally, I will share some popular fresh produce items you should avoid due to their high levels of contamination from pesticides.

## The Main Household Toxins

Following are the "top culprits" in polluting the air inside your home, along with their alternate names, where they are found, their toxic impact, and how you can mitigate their effects.

#### ACETONE

**Other names:** Dimethyl ketone, ketone propane, and 2-propanone.

**Where it's found:** Acetone is found in fingernail polish remover, glues, rubber cement, cleaners, and lacquers.

**Effects:** Acetone affects the nervous system, causing eye and nasal irritation, and impacts the cardiovascular, respiratory, and urinary systems.

## ALUMINUM
**Where it's found:** Aluminum is used in antiperspirants.

**Effects:** Aluminum creates toxicity in the body; has a detrimental effect on lungs and bones; and causes cell structures to malfunction, encouraging neurological diseases like Alzheimer's, dementia, and multiple sclerosis.

**Quick fix:** Use deodorant that utilizes alcohol to kill bacteria (thereby eliminating smell).

## AMMONIA
**Where it's found:** Ammonia is found in cleaners, textiles, dyes, plastics, rubber, glass cleaners, toilet bowl cleaners, pharmaceuticals, pesticides, leather, flame retardants, metal polishes, floor strippers, wax removers, smelling salts, and petroleum products.

**Effects:** Ammonia is linked to seizures, lung damage, asthma, dermatitis, blindness, coma, and death.

**Quick fix:** Use natural glass cleaners made with vinegar.

## BENZENE
**Other names:** Benzol, aniline, phenyl hydride, naphthalene, and naphtha (coal tar).

**Where it's found:** Benzene is found in chemical-based cleaners, paints, glues, plastics, detergents, furniture waxes, furniture polishes, cigarette smoke,

pesticides, lubricants, oven cleaners, spot removers, mothballs, and carpet cleaners.

**Effects:** Benzene is identified as a carcinogen by the U.S. Department of Health and Human Services and the International Agency for Research on Cancer. The 1990 Clean Air Act named it a hazardous pollutant, and it appears on the EPA's "Right-to-Know" list of hazardous substances. Benzene is linked to leukemia and disrupts kidney function, having its greatest effects on children.

**Quick fixes:**

- Leave the garage door open after using your car or other gas-powered motorized equipment, in order to ventilate the area.

- Choose products that are benzene-free.

### CHLORINE

**Other names:** Hypochlorite, sodium dichloroisocyanurate, hydrogen chloride, and hydrochloric acid.

**Where it's found:** Chlorine is found in the public water supply, pool water, bleach, disinfectants, and pesticides.

**Effects:** Chlorine is on the EPA's "Right-to-Know" list of hazardous substances, and the 1990 Clean Air Act recognized it as a hazardous pollutant. Chlorine is linked to some cancers, asthma, and lung damage. When mixed with ammonia (for example, when you use both a typical bathroom cleaner that contains chlorine and a typical glass cleaner that contains ammonia), the deadly concoction created is mustard gas.

**Quick fixes:**

- Limit your drinking of unfiltered water.

- Eliminate chlorine-based cleaning products from your home.

### Diethanolamine (DEA), Monoethanolamine (MEA), and Triethanolamine (TEA)

**Where they're found:** DEA, MEA, and TEA are found in shampoos, lotions, creams, cosmetics, and detergents.

**Effects:** DEA, MEA, and TEA are considered "safe with qualifications" in the United States, and their use is restricted in Europe. They are known carcinogens, increasing the occurrence of liver and kidney dysfunction and causing allergic reactions.

**Quick fix:** Avoid products that contain these chemicals, and choose organic products instead.

### Dioxin

**Where it's found:** Dioxin is found in coffee filters, bleached paper products, chlorine bleach, chlorophenol weed killers, wood preservatives, plastic wraps, PVC, and pesticides.

**Effects:** The International Agency for Research on Cancer classifies dioxin as a "Group 1" carcinogen, which means that it is definitely carcinogenic to humans. Ninety percent of human exposure is through food; levels are highest in food with the greatest percentage of fat. Agent Orange brought awareness to dioxin in the 1980s.

**Quick fixes:**

- Avoid bleached coffee filters.

- Trim fat from meat products.

- Avoid bleached paper products.

- Avoid plastic wraps.

## FORMALDEHYDE

**Other names:** Quaternium-15, 2-bromo-2-nitropropane-1, 3-diol, diazolidinyl urea, imidazolidinyl urea, and DMDM hydantoin.

**Where it's found:** Formaldehyde is found in paints, cleaning products, toilet paper, tissues, personal care products, car exhaust, foam insulation, plywood, particleboard, floorboard resins, synthetic carpet dyes, glues, pressed wood products (cabinetry, plywood paneling, and furniture), baby care products, liquid shower gels, body lotions, and bubble bath.

**Effects:** Formaldehyde damages DNA; interferes with the central nervous system; has a direct link to cancer; and is connected to asthma, joint pain, depression, headaches, chronic fatigue, and ear infections. Japan has banned formaldehyde in personal care products.

**Quick fixes:**

- Avoid home furnishings or cabinetry with particleboard.
- Choose personal care products that are organic.

## FRAGRANCE

**Where it's found:** Fragrance is found in cleaning products, personal care products, and candles. It is also pumped into retail stores and hotels.

**Effects:** Fragrance consists mainly of petroleum-based synthetic chemicals known to cause cancer, birth defects, central nervous system disorders, and allergic reactions.

**Quick fixes:**

- Read labels to make sure the products you use don't contain fragrance. Be aware that some companies *add* chemical fragrance *eliminators* to products in order to mask scent.

- Use essential oils if you are looking to create a mood with a specific scent.

## Nonylphenols

**Where they're found:** Nonylphenols are found in shampoos, shaving creams, detergents, cosmetics, wax used for fruits and vegetables, skin creams, hair dyes, plastic food packaging, spermicides, pesticides, paints, textiles, leather processing, and paper manufacturing.

**Effects:** Nonylphenols mimic the type of estrogen that is linked to estrogen-related cancer. The German government has banned nonylphenols.

**Quick fix:** Avoid products that contain this family of chemical compounds.

## Parabens

**Other names:** Methyl, propyl, butyl, and ethyl.

**Where they're found:** Parabens are found in cosmetics, toothpastes, shampoos, conditioners, moisturizers, personal care products, and food preservatives.

**Effects:** Parabens are absorbed through the skin and act like estrogen; they are linked to cancer. It is important for young girls and teenagers to stay away from products containing this chemical.

**Quick fix:** Stay away from products that have emergency warnings against swallowing or inhaling them.

### Perchlorethylene (PERC)

**Where it's found:** Eighty-five percent of dry cleaners use PERC.

**Effects:** The EPA classifies PERC as a probable carcinogen and has suggested that it be phased out by 2023. Some dry cleaners have begun to use DF-2000, which is petroleum-based, or EcoSolv; these dry cleaning fluids are also linked to health problems.

**Quick fixes:**

- Hang dry-cleaned garments outdoors (or in your garage) for two days to air out the chemicals.

- Find a dry cleaner who uses $CO_2$ cleaning or wet cleaning.

### Phthalates

**Other names:** Diethyl phthalate (DEP), DBP, DEHP, BzBP, and DMP.

**Where they're found:** Phthalates are found in plastics, PVC, fragrance powders, aftershaves, skin creams, hair products, synthetic clothing, flooring, and baby products (bottles, teething rings, and pacifiers).

**Effects:** Phthalates are known to cause liver cancer and to disrupt the endocrine (hormonal) system. They are associated with learning disabilities; severe attention deficit disorder; cognitive and brain development problems; breast cancer; prostate and testicular cancer;

thyroid cancer; and sexual development problems, including feminization of males.

**Quick fixes:**

- Avoid plastics unless they have the recycling code 1, 2, or 5.

- Avoid baby products that are made of plastic.

## POLYSORBATES 60 AND 80

**Other names:** Tween 80, polyoxyethylene (20), sorbitan monostearate, and polyoxyethylene (20) sorbitan monooleate.

**Where they're found:** Polysorbates are found in cosmetics, shampoos, baby lotions, scented powders, makeup foundations, exfoliants, sunless tanners, skin-cleansing creams, antiaging creams, artificial whipped cream, ice cream, salad dressings, Jell-O, pickle jars, baked goods, medicines, and vaccines.

**Effects:** Polysorbates cause infertility, reproductive issues, organ toxicity, and cancer.

**Quick fix:** Read labels on cosmetics and skin care products to avoid those with polysorbates. Because we use these products repetitively, it is important that they be free of toxins.

## POLYVINYL CHLORIDE (PVC)

**Other name:** Vinyl.

**Where it's found:** PVC is typically mixed with plasticizers (phthalates), stabilizers, flame retardants, and lubricants to make the PVC practical to use. These additives compound the toxicity. PVC is found in building materials, pipes, vinyl flooring, shower curtains, siding, wallpaper, furniture (plastic chairs), windows, food packaging, children's toys, plastic wraps, imitation leather, baby bottles, and pens.

**Effects:** PVC is carcinogenic and disrupts metabolism. It is linked to asthma, thyroid dysfunction, early puberty, reproductive issues, and allergies.

**Quick fixes:**

- Use real wood, ceramic, or stone tile for flooring.

- Choose natural furnishing products from companies renowned for Earth-friendly practices.

- Avoid plastic toys.

- Avoid meats packaged in plastic.

### Propylene Glycol (PG), Polyethylene Glycol (PEG), and Ethylene Glycol (EG)

**Where they're found:** PG, PEG, and EG are found in body lotions, deodorants, hair conditioners, hair gels, detanglers, cleansing creams, toners, baby powders, baby wipes, mouthwashes, toothpastes, suntan lotions, lipsticks, flavored coffees (as preservatives), processed foods, fabric softeners, stain removers, paints, adhesives, wallpaper strippers, rubber cleaners, de-icers, and degreasers.

**Effects:** The EPA warns factory workers to avoid skin contact with PG, PEG, and EG, in order to prevent brain, liver, and kidney damage. These chemicals are linked to skin damage, thickening of the skin, dermatitis, stunted growth, decreased blood pressure, and heart arrhythmia.

**Quick fixes:**

- Avoid stick-style deodorants, which have a higher concentration of PG than is allowed for industrial use. (The EPA requires workers to wear protective gear when working with PG.)

- Avoid mouthwash with more than 25 percent alcohol, which has been linked to tongue and throat cancer.

## TALC

**Where it's found:** Talc is found in pesticides, antacids, flea and tick powders, baby powders, cosmetics (blush, eye shadow, and face powder), chalks, crayons, medicated powders, perfumed powders, textiles, paper, paper processing, and food processing.

**Effects:** Minute fibers of talc have effects similar to asbestos. Talc is linked to lung cancer, ovarian cancer, and respiratory illness.

**Quick fixes:**

- Do not use baby powder.

- Find powdered cosmetics that do not include talc, or use liquid cosmetics.

## TOLUENE

**Other names:** Methylbenzene, phenylmethane, and toluol.

**Where it's found:** Toluene is a liquid found in waxes, adhesives, paints, paint thinners, medicines, dyes, detergents, fingernail polishes, spot removers, lacquers, adhesives, rubber, antifreeze, gasoline, exhaust, and the printing and leather-tanning processes.

**Effects:** Toluene has a negative impact on the kidneys, nervous system, liver, brain, and heart. It can cause birth defects, learning disabilities, hearing loss, permanent brain damage, and depression. The European Union banned toluene in cosmetic products in 2004. The United States doesn't require cosmetic products to be tested for safety.

**Quick fixes:**

- Keep the garage door open to ventilate exhaust fumes.

- Avoid cosmetics with toluene.

## TRICHLOROETHYLENE (TCE)

**Where it's found:** TCE is found in dry cleaning fluids, paint removers, varnishes, spot removers, rug cleaners, and decaffeinated coffee. It is also found in the public water supply; we drink this water, and we inhale TCE from the air during a shower or bath.

**Effects:** TCE is a carcinogen that also damages the nervous system, liver, and kidney. It irritates the eyes, throat, and skin.

**Quick fix:** Read labels and avoid products that contain TCE.

## TRICLOSAN

**Where it's found:** Triclosan is a synthetic antibacterial compound used in antibacterial soaps and gels, deodorants, body washes, cosmetics, toothpastes, cookware, furniture, toys, clothing, and acrylic fabrics.

**Effects:** The EPA considers triclosan a pesticide. It alters hormone regulation, contributes to antibiotic resistance, and disrupts thyroid function. It is linked to brain damage and learning disabilities, reproductive issues and infertility, and cancer.

**Quick fixes:**

- Avoid toothpaste that contains triclosan.

- Avoid antibacterial soaps, gels, and wipes.

## VOCs (VOLATILE ORGANIC COMPOUNDS)

**Other names:** Formaldehyde, benzene, and trichloroethylene.

**Where they're found:** VOCs are found in paints, adhesives, cleaning products, hairsprays, perfumes, dry cleaning fluids, nail polishes, carpets, synthetic carpet pads, PVC, wallpaper, furniture, bedding, flame retardants, synthetic dyes, and hygiene products (as fragrance).

**Effects:** VOCs cause eye irritation and visual disorders, respiratory tract problems, headaches, memory impairment, motor impairment, and liver and kidney damage. They disrupt the central nervous system and are linked to cancer.

**Quick fixes:**

- Make sure your home has adequate ventilation.

- Use air filters and plants to clean the air in your home.

- Remove toxic substances from sleeping areas to reduce the cumulative effect of VOCs.

- Avoid unnecessary pollution sources, like paints, adhesives, pesticides, and cleaning products. Replace these items with natural ones.

### XYLENE

**Where it's found:** Xylene is a solvent used in leather, rubber, printing, paints, varnishes, fingernail polishes, adhesives, rubber cement, gasoline, perfumes, pesticides, pharmaceuticals, polyester, plastics, and cleaning agents.

**Effects:** Xylene affects the central nervous system and can cause liver damage, kidney damage, loss of coordination, loss of consciousness, and respiratory failure.

**Quick fix:** Use plants to purify the air in your home.

## Toxins in Home Furnishings

This section refers to some of the household toxins described in the previous section, along with other noxious chemicals. For easy reference, these toxins—as well as ways to deal with them—are arranged according to where they are found in the home environment.

## PAINT

**Toxins:** Paint contains VOCs (volatile organic compounds) and possibly ammonia.

**Effects:** VOCs have been linked to cancer.

**Quick fixes:**

- Choose paint products with low or no VOCs.

- Ventilate painted areas by opening the windows and running fans until the smell of paint is gone.

## CARPET

**Toxins:** Synthetic carpets can emit VOCs (benzene and styrene) and other toxins for five years or more.

**Effects:** These toxins have been linked to lymphoma, leukemia, cognitive impairment, hearing loss, and cancer.

**Quick fixes:**

- Choose natural-fiber carpets like wool, sisal, seagrass, and jute.

- When you install new synthetic carpet, the EPA recommends ventilating the room with open windows and fans for at least 72 hours.

- On synthetic carpet, use a vacuum cleaner with a HEPA filter as well as a hot-water vacuum (steam cleaner).

## WALLPAPER AND ADHESIVES

**Toxins:** Many types of wallpaper and wallpaper adhesives contain PVC and phthalates.

**Effects:** These chemicals have been linked to asthma, birth defects, learning disabilities, liver damage, and cancer.

**Quick fixes:**

- Choose PVC-free wallpaper.

- Avoid vinyl wallpaper that contains phthalates.

- Choose natural-fiber-based wallpaper.

- Avoid wallpaper that contains synthetic inks or solvents.

- Avoid acrylic or vinyl-based glue adhesives; use water-based, water-soluble pastes.

- Seek out wallpaper made of grass and straw fibers; this type of wallpaper is inherently antimicrobial and mold-resistant.

- Choose products with GREENGUARD Certification to ensure that they have low chemical emissions.

## LIGHT BULBS AND ANTIQUE MIRRORS

**Toxin:** Mercury.

**Effects:** Mercury is known to cause vomiting, headaches, memory loss, high blood pressure, and muscle tremors.

**Quick fix:** Avoid having items that contain mercury, especially in places frequented by young children.

## SHOWER CURTAINS AND PLASTIC TABLECLOTHS

**Toxin:** Phthalates.

**Effects:** Phthalates are a known carcinogen and hormone disruptor. They can cause problems in cognition and brain development.

**Quick fixes:**

- Avoid soft plastics.

- Use shower curtains and tablecloths made of a natural fabric, like cotton or linen.

- If you can smell a product's off-gasses, don't buy it.

## PRESSED WOOD FURNITURE, CABINETRY, PARTICLEBOARD, PLYWOOD, MDF (MEDIUM-DENSITY FIBREBOARD), AND PERMANENT-PRESS FABRIC

**Toxin:** Formaldehyde, in high levels.

**Effects:** Formaldehyde is carcinogenic.

**Quick fixes:**

- If you can smell a product's off-gasses, don't buy it.

- Use formaldehyde-free lumber, gypsum board, and hardboard products; stainless steel and other metals; and adobe, bricks, tile, and other masonry.

- Use water-resistant sealants to lock in off-gasses.

- Seek out products that emit *less* formaldehyde, including those containing phenol formaldehyde (PF) resin or methylene diphenyl diisocyanate (MDI)

resin. One caveat regarding this advice is that while the EPA suggests the use of PF and MDI, other sources still consider these substances to be carcinogenic.

- Buy particleboard or hardwood plywood stamped with the Composite Panel Association (CPA) or Hardwood Plywood and Veneer Association (HPVA) seal of approval, to ensure lower formaldehyde emissions.

- Sometimes, manufacturers seal products on only one side. Check all sides of an item and seal them, if necessary. Or if you are ordering a custom item, specify that you want sealants on all surfaces.

### UREA-FORMALDEHYDE–BASED COATINGS ON FURNITURE, LAMINATE, SOLID WOOD FLOORS, AND CABINETRY

**Toxins:** VOCs, including high levels of formaldehyde.
**Effects:** VOCs are carcinogenic.
**Quick fixes:**

- Use the following finishes, which emit only low amounts of VOCs: acrylic coating, vinyl coating, melamine laminate, heat-curable two-component polyurethane, UV-curable acrylate, and UV-curable multifunctional acrylate.

- Because finishes emit VOCs during the curing and drying processes, it is important to ventilate the area well for several days after application.

## PERMANENT-PRESS TEXTILES IN DRAPERIES, CLOTHING, BEDDING, AND FURNITURE

**Toxin:** Formaldehyde.

**Effects:** Formaldehyde is a known carcinogen.

**Quick fixes:**

- Ask distributors of furnishings, draperies, and bedding to air out these products for a few days at their facility before you bring them into your home.

- Wash clothing, bedding, and other textiles before use to reduce formaldehyde by 60 percent. Always wash clothes before wearing.

## FLAME RETARDANTS IN CLOTHING, FURNITURE, FABRIC, CARPETING, AND COMPUTERS

**Toxins:** Flame-retardant chemicals.

**Effects:** The residual dust from flame retardants accumulates in homes and causes a host of health issues, including infertility, hormone disruption, behavioral issues in children, brain development problems, and cancer.

**Quick fixes:**

- When choosing rugs, draperies, and bedding, buy natural-fiber items that are inherently fire-resistant. Wool and linen are great choices.

- Buy upholstered furniture stuffed with wool, jute, or cotton.

- Because many of the particles we inhale are contained in the dust in our homes, it

is important to dust with a damp mop and use a vacuum cleaner with a HEPA filter.

- Avoid flame-retardant pajamas.

## STAIN PROTECTORS ON CARPETING, UPHOLSTERED FURNITURE, CLOTHING, AND FABRIC

**Toxin:** Perfluorinated chemicals (PFCs), which are applied to alleviate permanent stains.

**Effects:** PFCs are associated with liver damage, immune and endocrine dysfunction, infertility, developmental defects, and cancer.

**Quick fixes:**

- Always decline optional treatment with stain protectors when purchasing furniture or carpeting.

- Avoid stain protectors, and choose natural products instead.

## PLASTIC CONTAINERS (BABY BOTTLES, SIPPY CUPS, WATER BOTTLES, FOOD STORAGE) AND COOKWARE

**Toxins:** Bisphenol A (BPA), polyvinyl chloride (PVC), polystyrene (Styrofoam), polytetrafluoroethylene (Teflon), perfluorooctanoic acid (PFOA), and low-density polyethylene (LDPE).

**Effects:** BPA and polystyrene are linked to cancer. The manufacturing process for PVC produces chemical compounds that can cause cancer; endocrine disruption; endometriosis; neurological damage; birth defects and impaired child development; and reproductive and immune system damage. In certain conditions, the Teflon coating on nonstick cookware releases PFOA, which is linked to a range of health problems, including cancer; infertility in women; and liver, immune system, developmental, and reproductive problems. The chemicals in Teflon, including PFOA, are considered likely to be carcinogenic to humans. LDPE has been connected to breast cancer.

**Quick fixes:**

- Choose stainless steel, cast iron, or enameled pots and pans.

- Make sure plastic containers say they are BPA-free.

- Use glass or stainless steel storage containers and bottles.

- Avoid canned goods that are lined with BPA and opt for dry goods (like bean products) instead.

- Avoid food products, such as eggs, that are packaged in Styrofoam.

- Avoid plastic wraps, and never microwave food that is covered by plastic wrap.

## Quick Reference Guide to Household Toxins

The following tables tell you, at a glance, the toxic ingredients found in common cleaning products, personal care products, and household items. Based on this information, you can make informed choices about what you bring into your home.

## Toxins in Cleaning Products

| Products | Ingredient(s) | Other Name(s) |
|---|---|---|
| All-purpose cleaners | Ammonia, bleach, propylene glycol (PG) | Hypochlorite, sodium dichloroisocyanurate, hydrogen chloride, hydrochloric acid |
| Carpet cleaners | Benzene, fragrance | Benzol, benzole, aniline, phenyl hydride, naphtha (coal tar), naphthalene, parfum |
| Dishwashing detergents | Chlorine, organic solvents, nonylphenols | Toluene, methylene chloride, trichloroethylene, hypochlorite, sodium dichloroisocyanurate, hydrogen chloride, hydrochloric acid |
| Drainage liquids | Bleach | Hypochlorite, sodium dichloroisocyanurate, hydrogen chloride, hydrochloric acid |
| Fabric softeners | Propylene glycol, fragrance | Parfum |
| Furniture polishes | Benzene, fragrance | Benzol, benzole, aniline, phenyl hydride, naphtha (coal tar), naphthalene, parfum |
| Glass cleaners | Ammonia, bleach | Hypochlorite, sodium dichloroisocyanurate, hydrogen chloride, hydrochloric acid |

| Products | Ingredient(s) | Other Name(s) |
|---|---|---|
| Laundry detergents | Benzene, non-ylphenols, organic solvents, ragrance | Benzol, benzole, aniline, phenyl hydride, naphtha (coal tar), naphthalene, toluene, methylene chloride, trichloroethylene, parfum |
| Metal polishes (stainless steel) | Ammonia, benzene | Benzol, benzole, aniline, phenyl hydride, naphtha (coal tar), naphthalene |
| Oven cleaners | Benzene | Benzol, benzole, aniline, phenyl hydride, naphtha (coal tar), naphthalene |
| Stain removers | Propylene glycol, benzene | Benzol, benzole, aniline, phenyl hydride, naphtha (coal tar), naphthalene |
| Toilet bowl cleaners | Ammonia, bleach | Hypochlorite, sodium dichloroisocyanurate, hydrogen chloride, hydrochloric acid |

## Toxins in Personal Care Products

| Products | Ingredient(s) | Other Name(s) |
|---|---|---|
| Antibacterial products | Bacteriocides, fragrance | Triclosan, benzalkonium chloride, chlorhexidine, parfum |
| Deodorants | Aluminum, phthalates, fragrance, talc | Aluminum chlorohydrate, aluminum zirconium, PEG, PG, EG, DBP, DEHP, BzBP, DMP, parfum |

| Products | Ingredient(s) | Other Name(s) |
|---|---|---|
| Face and body lotions | Mineral oils, silicones, preservatives, thickening agents, emulsifiers, phthalates, formaldehyde, parabens, nonylphenols, fragrance | Parabens, EDTA, formaldehyde, methylisothiazolinone, paraffinum liquidum, petrolatum, cyclomethicone, dimethicone, simethicone, cyclopentasiloxane, DEA, TEA, MEA, PEG, PG, EG, diazolidinyl urea, imidazolidinyl urea, nonylphenols, quaternium-15, 2-bromo-2-nitropropane-1, 3-diol, DMDM hydantoin, DBP, DEHP, BzBP, DMP, parfum |
| Hairsprays | Phthalates, fragrance | DBP, DEHP, parfum |
| Perfumed products | Fragrance | Parfum |
| Powders and talc | Talc | Powder |
| Shampoos, body washes, and shaving products | Detergents, nonylphenols, parabens, phthalates, preservatives, formaldehyde, fragrance | Sodium lauryl sulfate, cocamidopropyl betaine, ammonium lauryl sulfate, cocamide DEA, cocamide MEA, nonylphenols, Tween 80, polyoxyethylene (20), sorbitan monostearate, polyoxyethylene (20) sorbitan monooleate, quaternium-15, 2-bromo-2-nitropropane-1, 3-diol, diazolidinyl urea, imidazolidinyl urea, DMDM hydantoin, DBP, DEHP, BzBP, DMP, parfum |

| Products | Ingredient(s) | Other Name(s) |
|---|---|---|
| Sun care products | Sunscreens, benzene | Benzophenone-3, homosalate, 4-MBC, octyl methoxycinnamate, octyl dimethyl PABA, octocrylene, benzol, benzole, aniline, phenyl hydride, naphtha (coal tar), naphthalene |

## Toxins in Household Items

| Product(s) | Ingredient(s) | Other Name(s) |
|---|---|---|
| Bedding | Formaldehyde, flame retardant, organic solvents, nonylphenols | Quaternium-15, 2-bromo-2-nitropropane-1, 3-diol, diazolidinyl urea, imidazolidinyl urea, DMDM hydantoin, toluene, methylene chloride, trichloroethylene |
| Carpeting | Formaldehyde, flame retardant, phthalates | DBP, DEHP, BzBP, DMP, 2-bromo-2-nitropropane-1, 3-diol, quaternium-15, diazolidinyl urea, imidazolidinyl urea, DMDM hydantoin |
| Fabric | Formaldehyde, nonylphenols | Quaternium-15, 2-bromo-2-nitropropane-1, 3-diol, diazolidinyl urea, imidazolidinyl urea, DMDM hydantoin |
| Flame retardants | Ammonia | |
| Furniture | Formaldehyde | Quaternium-15, 2-bromo-2-nitropropane-1, 3-diol, diazolidinyl urea, imidazolidinyl urea, DMDM hydantoin |

| Products | Ingredient(s) | Other Name(s) |
|---|---|---|
| Leather | Ammonia, formaldehyde, nonylphenols | Quaternium-15, 2-bromo-2-nitropropane-1, 3-diol, diazolidinyl urea, imidazolidinyl urea, DMDM hydantoin |
| Particleboard (MDF) | Formaldehyde | Quaternium-15, 2-bromo-2-nitropropane-1, 3-diol, diazolidinyl urea, imidazolidinyl urea, DMDM hydantoin |

## Toxic Fruits and Vegetables

You can enjoy the health benefits of a diet rich in fruits and vegetables by avoiding the most pesticide-ridden produce and buying organic instead. (In organic farming, biological pest control is used.) The idea is to reduce your exposure to pesticides as much as possible. Every year, the Environmental Working Group releases a list of the most pesticide-contaminated fruits and vegetables. Following is an excerpt from EWG's latest rankings, starting with the *most* toxic.[1]

Apples
Strawberries
Grapes
Celery
Peaches
Spinach
Sweet bell peppers
Nectarines (imported)
Cucumbers
Potatoes
Cherry tomatoes
Hot peppers

Blueberries (domestic)
Lettuce
Snap peas (imported)
Kale and collard greens
Cherries
Nectarines (domestic)
Pears
Plums
Raspberries
Blueberries (imported)
Carrots
Green beans

## *Choices for a Healthy Home*

I have already provided some quick fixes for dealing with common household toxins. In this section, I will give you specific recommendations for healthful items to bring into your home, including air-purifying plants and nontoxic cleaning products, personal care products, and groceries.

# Plants That Filter the Air

In the late 1980s, NASA and the Associated Landscape Contractors of America performed studies to determine whether typical houseplants could help clean the air in ground-based space facilities. They found that common plants were able to purify the air of VOCs and other noxious chemical compounds. Specifically, plants do the following:

- Help naturally clean and purify the air
- "Breathe in" and absorb toxins through their leaves
- Re-oxygenate the air by turning $CO_2$ (carbon dioxide) into oxygen

For beneficial results, use one or two potted plants per 100 square feet. Please refer to the following table for plants to help with specific chemicals found in the average home.

# Plants for Counteracting Specific Toxins

| Toxin | Recommended Plant(s) |
|---|---|
| Ammonia | Lady palm (Rhapis excelsa) |
| Benzene | English ivy (Hedera helix), Madagascar dragon tree or red-edged dracaena (Dracaena marginata), Janet Craig (Dracaena deremensis), chrysanthemum, Gerbera daisy, aloe, spider plant, bamboo palm or reed palm (Chamaedorea seifrizii), snake plant or mother-in-law's tongue (Sansevieria trifasciata or Sansevieria laurentii), golden pothos, wax begonia |
| Carbon monoxide | Spider plant, golden pothos |
| Formaldehyde | Azalea, dieffenbachia, philodendron, spider plant, golden pothos, bamboo palm or reed palm (Chamaedorea seifrizii), corn plant, chrysanthemum, snake plant or mother-in-law's tongue (Sansevieria trifasciata or Sansevieria laurentii), Madagascar dragon tree or red-edged dracaena (Dracaena marginata), weeping fig (Ficus benjamina), English ivy (Hedera helix), Boston fern |
| Toluene | Peace lily (Spathiphyllum), wax begonia |
| Trichloroethylene (TCE) | Gerbera daisy, chrysanthemum, peace lily (Spathiphyllum), Warneckii (Dracaena deremensis), Madagascar dragon tree or red-edged dracaena (Dracaena marginata), weeping fig (Ficus benjamina), bamboo palm or reed palm (Chamaedorea seifrizii) |
| Various | The Chinese evergreen (Aglaonema crispum var. deborah) is a "super plant" that removes a variety of contaminants from the air and clears more toxins as time and exposure increase. |

| Toxin | Recommended Plant(s) |
|---|---|
| Volatile organic compounds (VOCs) | Heart-leaf philodendron (Philodendron oxycardium) |
| Xylene | Spider plant, Madagascar dragon tree or red-edged dracaena (Dracaena marginata), weeping fig (Ficus benjamina) |

## Recommended Cleaning Products

To avoid the ammonia, bleach, chlorine, benzene, fragrance, and other toxins found in most household cleaners, please refer to the following table of safer options.

### Suggested Household Cleaners

| Products | Recommendations |
|---|---|
| Bathroom cleaners | Ecover Ecological Bathroom Cleaner; Simple Green Naturals Bathroom Cleaner; CLR Calcium, Lime & Rust Remover; Seventh Generation Natural Tub & Tile Cleaner (Emerald Cypress & Fir) |
| Dishwashing detergents | Seventh Generation Natural Dishwasher Detergent, Earth Friendly Products DuoDish (Organic Lavender) |
| Laundry detergents and fabric softeners | GreenShield Organic Laundry Detergent, Martha Stewart Clean Laundry Detergent, GreenShield Organic Fabric Softener (Lavender Mint) |
| Wood floor and furniture cleaners | Method Wood for Good Daily Clean, Almond Citra Solv Wood Natural Wood & Furniture Polish (Valencia Orange) |

## Recommended Personal Care Products

The skin is the human body's largest organ. According to Dr. Theresa Ramsey, we absorb 60 percent of whatever is put on our skin[2] (which is why topical medications are used). What is applied to the skin finds its way into the bloodstream. Therefore, you must choose safe cosmetics and other personal care products, like the ones in the following table.

### Suggested Personal Care Products

| Product | Recommendation(s) |
| --- | --- |
| Bar soap | Kiss My Face Pure Olive Oil Soap, Aubrey Organics Bath Bar, Baby Hugo Naturals Handcrafted Soap (for baby) |
| Blush | bareMinerals |
| Conditioner | Desert Essence Tea Tree Replenishing Conditioner (with Peppermint and Yucca), Hugo Naturals Smoothing & Defining Conditioner (Coconut) |
| Deodorant | Tom's of Maine roll-on deodorant, Nourish Organic Deodorant |
| Facial cleanser | Annmarie Gianni Skin Care Aloe-Herb Cleanser |
| Lipstick | Coastal Classic Creations |
| Liquid hand soap | Kiss My Face Peace Soap |
| Makeup remover | Blum Naturals |
| Moisturizer | Hugo Naturals Unscented Body Butter, John Masters Organics Hand & Body Butter |

| Product | Recommendation(s) |
|---|---|
| Pressed powder | bareMinerals, Mineralz, Maybelline Fit Me, L'Oreal Visible Lift Serum Absolute |
| Shampoo | Hugo Naturals, Desert Essence Organics Shampoo (with Peppermint and Yucca, Lemon Tea Tree, or Fragrance Free) |
| Toothpaste | Kiss My Face Kids Toothpaste (without fluoride), Xlear Spry Toothpaste with Xylitol (Fluoride Free), Tom's of Maine Fluoride-Free Baking Soda Toothpaste |

## Grocery Suggestions

When you begin to adopt a clean-eating lifestyle, shopping can feel overwhelming. The following lists of recommended pantry items, fruits and vegetables, spices, and smoothie ingredients can give you some direction.

### Pantry Items

Organic olive oil
Organic cannellini beans
Organic chickpeas
Organic red kidney beans
Organic dark red kidney
    beans
Organic black kidney
    beans
Organic pasta sauce
Organic pizza sauce
Organic crushed
    tomatoes
Organic hearts of palm
Organic quinoa

### Produce

Organic carrots
Organic cucumbers
Organic avocados
Organic baby arugula
Organic baby spinach
Organic romaine
Organic kale
Organic bell peppers
Organic berries
Organic seasonal fruit
Organic seasonal
    vegetables
Organic eggs

## Spices

| | |
|---|---|
| Himalayan sea salt in a salt mill (grinder) | Organic ground mustard seed |
| Organic black peppercorns in a pepper mill (grinder) | Organic rosemary |
| | Organic coriander |
| Organic turmeric | Organic ground cumin |
| | Organic celery seed |

## Smoothie Essentials

| | |
|---|---|
| Organic vanilla protein powder | Organic coconut water |
| Organic cacao powder | Vanilla coconut milk |
| Organic ground flaxseeds | Frozen organic fruit |
| | Organic bananas |

# Appendix B

# Inspired Party Ideas and Vibrant-Living Recipes

To ease your transition to the Home in Harmony Lifestyle, in this section, I will provide healthy recipes that utilize many of the nutrient-dense superfoods we discussed earlier. These recipes are arranged in menus for entertaining, but you can easily incorporate them into your daily routine. After all, healthy living is important whether you are curled up on your couch or hosting an event for your family and friends! First, I will give you some easy tips for making any party a success—and decreasing your stress as the host.

## Ten Tips to Make Your Party a Success!

Every year, we welcome 200 guests through our front door for our annual holiday party, to toast the season of light. I am delighted to share my secrets for successfully (and effortlessly!) hosting a party of up to 200 people. The following suggestions will allow you to enjoy your gathering and move through it with ease and grace.

1. *Make a list.* Staying organized, focused, and on task will help relieve the pressure that can be associated with having a party. Allow enough time to get everything done, because it is better to have too much time than to "burn the midnight oil" right before the event—leaving you drained and exhausted for your own party. Make a list of all the items you are going to need, identifying which ones you will purchase and which ones you will make. Your list of party components might include the following:

- *Food.* Plan the style of food you want to serve, such as dinner, or heavy appetizers with petit fours.

- *Utensils.* Based on the menu, determine the types of plates, silverware, and serving pieces you will need.

- *Drinks.* Identify the kinds of drinks you will serve and plan for appropriate mixers and cups. If you offer coffee and tea, you will need mugs, creamer, and sweetener.

- *Decorations.* Decide on the party's theme and how you are going to enhance the event with decorations. Your embellishments may be as simple as a few candles, for ambience.

Put a time line together of what you are going to accomplish on which days. Mapping out your to-dos will help you to stay on schedule and alleviate the stress of hosting a gathering.

2. *Select the right music.* Music is a key element in generating the atmosphere of a party; it has a direct impact on people's moods. Prepare your playlist ahead of time, taking into account the general feeling you want to create.

3. *Arrange food in stations.* Set up different stations, or areas where food will be served. This layout will allow the party to flow and encourage people to circulate from one place to another. Position the bar where it will help people mingle away from a central location that might be more congested.

4. *Prepare serving pieces.* Know what serving pieces you are going to use for each dish, so you don't have to do any frantic guessing during the party. Take out the utensils for each item. Set the table, including any decorations, the day before.

5. *Plan the timing of food.* Make a list of the dishes that need to go into the oven and work out the timing. For example, cook the baked brie and the artichoke dip together because they require the same temperature. Know that you will put these items in the oven 30 minutes before the party starts, so they can be served piping hot. Decide when dessert will come out and where it will

be placed. If the flow of food is scheduled, you won't stress about it during the party.

6. *Develop a system for handling coats.* Where are you going to put coats, who will put them there, and how will guests retrieve them at the end of the night? For a recent party, I put my 12-year-old and a few of her friends in charge of coats when guests arrived. The kids were instructed to place coats from the same family on the same hanger, if possible. This technique makes it easier for guests to get their items on the way out and reduces the risk of mixing up coats.

7. *Set up conversation areas.* Don't be afraid to move the furniture. Arrange seating so that it is conducive to conversations of both larger and smaller groups, in both more crowded areas and less congested spots. This setup allows guests to find the location where they are most comfortable, depending on whether they want to be "in the mix" or have a quiet conversation.

8. *Include a "signature something."* Taking the time to put your special touch on your party will make it an event to remember. Come up with something that people will think back fondly on for years to come. At our annual holiday party, we serve our signature gingerbread martini, which gets rave reviews. Everyone always wants the recipe and talks about it until the following year!

9. *Send guests off with a party favor to remember.* Find or make a little item that you can give your guests upon their departure—something that will help them remember the event. It can be as simple as a small bag

of homemade fudge or as elaborate as a hand-crafted ornament. Offering such a token is a way to show your gratitude for your guests' participation in the gathering!

10. *Take a deep breath.* Plan to take a few minutes before your guests arrive to breathe deeply and enjoy the festive atmosphere you have created. My husband and I always allow ourselves 20 minutes before a party to set the mood lighting, dance to the music, and toast to another great soiree.

Preparing ahead lets you relax and enjoy your own party, whether you are entertaining 10 or 200. Greet each guest with a smile and celebrate! Happy entertaining!

### Festive Ideas and Themes

Let's look at some fun concepts for your upcoming gatherings, which you thought only Martha Stewart could pull together with such a perfect touch! We will incorporate healthy recipes to ensure that you are nourishing yourself, your family, and your guests. In these dishes, and in all of your cooking, be sure to use organic ingredients whenever possible.

## The Festive Mingle

When throwing a party where guests can mingle and chat, it is important to take a few things into consideration. Plan munchies that are easy to handle and won't end up on the floor. Make your festive food bite-size, so your guests can enjoy conversing while eating.

For a more formal affair, you can place dips and spreads on small toast points or gluten-free rice crackers. Offering veggies for dipping is a healthier option. Mindfully choosing fare that will help your guests avoid stress and strain creates a harmonious atmosphere—one that encourages socializing and partaking in food that is nourishing and nurturing. Your guests will be able to dexterously mix the "mingle" with the "munch." As one who frequents parties, I am always perplexed as to how to clasp my purse, hold a cocktail, and accept an hors d'oeuvre and napkin while simultaneously carrying on a conversation. I have learned through the years to have my husband hold my lipstick in his pocket so I don't need to bring a clutch.

## HOME IN HARMONY SEASONING BLEND

I use this seasoning blend in virtually everything I cook. It works well with eggs and in dips, soup bases, and veggie sautés. Sometimes, I just add a dash to a dish of olive oil for delicious dipping.

Coarse Himalayan sea salt
Organic black peppercorns
Organic coriander seeds
Organic dried rosemary
Organic white peppercorns
Organic caraway seeds

Fill a glass peppermill with equal parts of the ingredients. Leave room at the top to be able to shake and mix the ingredients.

## GUACAMOLE

3 organic Hass avocados, separated from their skins and mashed

Juice of 1 organic lime (adding a little pulp will provide some extra zest)

1 teaspoon Home in Harmony Seasoning Blend

1 teaspoon organic ground cumin

¼ teaspoon organic chili powder

Combine the ingredients.

## WHITE BEAN DIP

2 cans organic great northern, cannellini, or garbanzo beans, rinsed

½ cup organic extra virgin olive oil

2 pinches coarse Himalayan sea salt

1 teaspoon Home in Harmony Seasoning Blend

2 pinches organic dried rosemary

2 pinches organic black peppercorns

1 tablespoon organic turmeric

Juice of half an organic lemon

In a food processor or other similar kitchen device, blend the ingredients until smooth or the desired texture.

## ROASTED RED PEPPER TAPENADE

1 7-ounce jar roasted red peppers, drained

1 6-ounce jar artichoke hearts, drained

¼ cup fresh lemon juice (organic)

1 3-ounce jar capers

½ cup grated parmesan cheese (optional)

Fresh organic parsley, for garnish

Place the red peppers and artichoke hearts in a food processor and pulse until the desired texture is achieved. Add the lemon juice, capers, and parmesan cheese (optional); pulse to mix. Garnish with parsley.

## Souper Supper

The "Souper Supper" theme is great for a cold-weather gathering. When we lived in a town in the Connecticut River Valley, one of our neighbors would invite us each year to a bring-your-own-soup (BYOS) party. Guests would bring a large pot of soup, stew, or chili to share with the group. As dinner approached, the host would ask us to share what our soup was, the ingredients that went into it, and how the dish had become part of our culinary repertoire. Each person would also bring index cards with the recipe written on them for the other guests. The varied culinary expressions were so unique! It was a fabulous way to try things you might not typically make in your own kitchen.

When preparing for this type of gathering, either designate a few people to bring bread and dessert, or cover this detail yourself. Make sure you have enough soup bowls, ladles, and soup spoons for everyone. Our host in Connecticut had trays that accommodated multiple bowls, to allow you to sample a selection of soups at once. However, trays aren't necessary. When I have hosted this type of party, I have provided larger bowls so that people could really enjoy their preferred soup. Remember to have plenty of napkins on hand for the spills that are inevitable when soup is served.

## CHRISTA'S CHILI

I always make a double batch of this chili to share with family or friends who might be in need of a home-cooked meal. Or I freeze the extra for when I am short on time but want to give my family something nutritious. This recipe is the double-batch version. Cut it in half if it is too much for you.

This recipe is the first of several in this appendix calling for canola oil, and I would like to make a few clarifications. First, be sure to use expeller-pressed organic canola oil. Second, make certain that the canola oil you use is verified non-GMO or non-GE. (These designations mean the same thing, that the oil has not been genetically modified or engineered.) I prefer canola oil to olive oil when cooking with medium heat, such as in sautéing onions, because canola oil has a higher smoke point than olive oil. That is, it can be heated to a higher temperature before unhealthy compounds form.

4 tablespoons expeller-pressed organic canola oil
Pinch coarse Himalayan sea salt
¼ teaspoon organic cinnamon
¼ teaspoon organic nutmeg
½ teaspoon organic allspice
4 teaspoons organic ground cumin
½ teaspoon organic chili powder
1 organic onion, finely chopped
3 pounds ground turkey (or grass-fed beef, if you have low iron levels)
4 28-ounce cans organic crushed tomatoes
2 6-ounce cans organic tomato paste (optional, for thicker chili)
6 15-ounce cans organic dark red kidney beans, red kidney beans, or black beans (or a desired combination)

Heat the oil. Add the salt, cinnamon, nutmeg, allspice, cumin, and chili powder; heat for one minute. Add the onion and sauté over medium heat until slightly browned and softened. Add the turkey and cook through. Add the tomatoes, tomato paste (optional), and beans. Heat on medium-low until the beans are tender, approximately 35 minutes. The chili gets better and better the longer it sits on the stove and simmers.

## HEARTY WHITE BEAN STEW

2 tablespoons expeller-pressed organic canola oil
2 cups finely chopped yellow onion (organic)
2 cloves organic garlic, minced
1 tablespoon organic ground cumin
1 teaspoon organic oregano
1 teaspoon organic ground coriander
2 teaspoons Home in Harmony Seasoning Blend
2 pounds cooked rotisserie chicken breasts (boneless, skinless, and shredded)
1 32-ounce carton organic chicken broth
4 cans organic cannellini beans

In a large stockpot, add the oil, onion, garlic, and spices. Sauté until the onion is translucent and tender. Add the chicken and toss to coat and warm. Add the chicken broth and beans. Simmer for 2 hours. The beans should be tender.

## KIELBASA AND CHICKPEA STEW

4 tablespoons expeller-pressed organic canola oil
1 teaspoon Home in Harmony Seasoning Blend
Pinch organic ground black pepper

Pinch organic crushed red pepper flakes
1 large organic elephant garlic, minced
1 organic onion, finely chopped
1 pound turkey kielbasa, cut into quarter-inch slices
2 8-ounce jars red peppers (strained and chopped)
8 cups organic chicken broth
3 cans organic chickpeas, rinsed
¾ cup frozen organic early peas
2 10-ounce containers organic hummus (preferably 1 plain and 1 red pepper)
8 ounces orzo or quinoa (or a quantity you prefer)

In a large stockpot or skillet with deep sides, heat the oil, spices, garlic, and onion. When the onions are translucent, add the kielbasa and red peppers. Sauté until the kielbasa is lightly browned. Add the chicken broth, chickpeas, and peas. Stir in the hummus. In a separate pot, cook orzo or quinoa. Continue to simmer the kielbasa and chickpeas while the orzo or quinoa is cooking. When the orzo or quinoa is done, add it to the large stockpot.

## MOM'S CHICKEN SOUP WITH QUINOA, RICE, OR PASTA

4 tablespoons expeller-pressed organic canola oil
2 pinches coarse Himalayan sea salt
4 teaspoons Home in Harmony Seasoning Blend
Bunch fresh organic dill, finely chopped
1 large organic yellow onion, diced
3 cloves organic garlic, minced
Bunch organic celery (5 or 6 stalks), diced
6 organic carrots, peeled and diced
4 organic parsnips, peeled and diced

1 or 2 tablespoons organic chicken broth
3 pounds boneless chicken breasts
3 32-ounce boxes organic chicken broth
1 pound uncooked noodles or 2½ cups uncooked
brown rice or 2 cups uncooked quinoa

In a large stockpot, heat the oil, salt, Home in Harmony
Seasoning Blend, and dill. Add the onion and garlic, and
cook until the onions are translucent. Add the celery,
carrots, and parsnips; cover and cook until al dente. Add
1 or 2 tablespoons chicken broth, if necessary, so that
the ingredients don't burn. After the vegetables are al
dente, add the 96 ounces of chicken broth. In a separate
pot, boil the chicken until it is cooked through; save
the chicken broth in case you need extra liquid later.
Cube the chicken into bite-sized pieces and add it to the
stockpot. In a separate pot, cook the noodles (until they
are al dente), brown rice, or quinoa; add to the stockpot.
Continue to simmer to allow the flavors to blend.

## Ladies' (or Gents') Harmony
## Brunch or Lunch

The "Harmony" brunch or lunch is equally suitable
for ladies and gentlemen. I have served this menu for a
midday affair on a variety of occasions. It includes one
of my favorite salmon recipes. In our house, there is a
gender bias regarding this protein. The ladies outnumber
the gentlemen, so by democratic process, salmon makes
its way to the table every so often. The ample health
benefits of salmon, which we discussed earlier, make it
an important food to include in everyone's diet. Even

my husband, who is not a huge fan of fish (especially the pink variety), likes the Orange Salmon dish below.

## ORANGE SALMON

2 large organic oranges, sliced thin into a wheel shape
½ large organic onion, sliced
1½ tablespoons organic olive oil
Home in Harmony Seasoning Blend, to taste
½ cup fresh orange juice (organic)
Juice of 1 organic lemon
2 tablespoons fresh organic dill, chopped
2 pounds wild salmon, bones and skin removed
1 tablespoon orange zest (organic)

We prefer to grill this dish, but you can also cook it in a baking dish in a 400-degree oven using the same steps.

Place the orange slices in a single layer on a grill pan (or you can create a pan using layers of tinfoil), and put the sliced onions on top. Drizzle olive oil and grind Home in Harmony Seasoning Blend over the top. Grill until the onions begin to brown.

In a sauté pan, heat the orange juice, lemon juice, and 1 tablespoon of the dill until simmering. Reserve the liquid and be prepared to pour 3 tablespoons of it onto the salmon while cooking so that it doesn't dry out. The remaining liquid can be served with the salmon.

On the grill pan, push the orange slices to the side. Place the salmon on the pan. Replace the orange slices on top of the salmon, using a spoon. Sprinkle with Home in Harmony Seasoning Blend, the remaining 1 tablespoon of dill, and the orange zest. Heat the salmon until it is cooked to the desired temperature. We prefer our salmon

medium-well, but I understand some people like theirs to be pink on the inside.

## EGG, TURKEY, AND RED PEPPER SAUTÉ

1 pound ground turkey
Home in Harmony Seasoning Blend, to taste
1 cup organic spinach, chopped
1 cup organic yellow and red peppers, diced
6 large organic eggs

Heat the turkey in a medium skillet until cooked through and slightly browned. Drain any excess liquid. Place the turkey in a bowl. Spray the pan with organic cooking spray. Heat the pan and add Home in Harmony Seasoning Blend. Add the vegetables and toss; cook until soft. Remove the vegetables and place them in the bowl with the turkey. Wipe the pan clean. Spray the pan with organic cooking spray. Add Home in Harmony Seasoning Blend. Thoroughly whip the eggs and add them to the heated pan. Toss the eggs, for an even scramble. When the eggs are almost fully cooked, add the turkey and veggies and toss.

## SCRUMPTIOUS EGG, AVOCADO, AND QUINOA

This recipe serves one person. Multiply the ingredients to serve larger groups. I use this recipe in one variation or another every day. It is especially yummy spread on rye toast that has been drizzled with olive oil and sprinkled with Home in Harmony Seasoning Blend.

2 large organic eggs

1 organic avocado

2 heaping tablespoons quinoa

Home in Harmony Seasoning Blend, to taste

Boil the eggs for 12 to 15 minutes, peel them, and place them in a bowl. Remove the avocado from its skin, discard the pit, and place the avocado in the bowl with the eggs. Add the quinoa. Add Home in Harmony Seasoning Blend, to taste. Chop and toss.

## BROCCOLI SAUTÉ

4 tablespoons expeller-pressed organic canola oil

1 teaspoon coarse Himalayan sea salt

2 teaspoons Home in Harmony Seasoning Blend

1 pound organic broccoli, chopped

In a large sauté pan, heat the oil and spices. Add the broccoli; toss to coat. Cover and cook until the desired tenderness is achieved. This will depend on the size of the broccoli. Our family likes broccoli al dente, which takes about 5 minutes.

## ARUGULA AND BROWN RICE SAUTÉ

4 tablespoons expeller-pressed organic canola oil

Pinch coarse Himalayan sea salt

2 teaspoons Home in Harmony Seasoning Blend

6 cups organic baby arugula

1 20-ounce bag frozen organic brown rice

1 tablespoon Bragg Liquid Aminos

In a large sauté pan, add the oil and spices. Add the arugula and toss to coat. Cover for 2 minutes. Add the

rice and Bragg Liquid Aminos. Stir and cook until the rice is heated through.

## SALAD WITH LEMON "KIDS' DELUXE" SALAD DRESSING

A colorful salad makes me smile. In this version, I cut colorful veggies into confetti-size pieces so that the salad looks like the celebration it is! When I worked at Chili's while I was in graduate school, I heard the term *confetti* referring to small pepper pieces on a pasta dish. I always thought that particular dish looked beautiful and festive. Every meal should be a beautiful celebration of abundance.

1 bag organic romaine hearts, rinsed and chopped
1 large organic cucumber, diced into small pieces with the skin on
1 organic red pepper, diced into confetti-size pieces
1 organic yellow pepper, diced into confetti-size pieces
1 organic orange pepper, diced into confetti-size pieces

Combine the ingredients and toss with Lemon "Kids' Deluxe" Salad Dressing.

## LEMON "KIDS' DELUXE" SALAD DRESSING

My kids really love this easy-to-prepare dressing.

½ cup organic extra virgin olive oil (EVOO)
Juice of 1 organic lemon
1 teaspoon Home in Harmony Seasoning Blend
3 splashes Tabasco Sauce

Combine the ingredients well.

# Harmony Smoothies and Juices

Smoothies and juices provide an easy, fun, and flavorful way to add fruits, vegetables, and abundant nutrients to your daily diet. They are great to "grab and go." Following are the ingredients for a few of our family favorites. To make these delicious and nutritious smoothies, combine the ingredients in a blender or Vitamix. Blend at high speed until the ingredients, including ice, are smooth.

## MORNING SHAKE

10 ice cubes
1 heaping tablespoon organic ground flaxseeds
1 heaping tablespoon organic vanilla rice protein powder
1 heaping tablespoon organic cacao powder
1 can organic coconut water

## KIDS' FAVORITE AFTER-SCHOOL BLUEBERRY, BANANA, AND CHOCOLATE SMOOTHIE

5 ice cubes
8 ounces frozen organic blueberries
1 ripe organic banana
1 heaping teaspoon organic cacao powder
1 heaping teaspoon organic ground flaxseeds
1 heaping teaspoon organic chia seeds
1 heaping teaspoon organic vanilla rice protein powder
3 cups vanilla coconut milk

## BANANA PEANUT BUTTER CUP SMOOTHIE
10 ice cubes
1 organic banana
½ cup organic peanuts or 1 tablespoon organic peanut butter (Whole Foods' 365 Organic Peanut Butter is a good choice)
1 heaping tablespoon organic cacao powder
2 cups vanilla coconut milk or almond milk

## RED AND GREEN SMOOTHIE
5 ice cubes
Heaping handful organic spinach
8 ounces frozen organic cherries
1 tablespoon organic cacao powder
1 tablespoon organic chia seeds
1 overripe organic banana
3 cups vanilla coconut milk

## GREEN GOODNESS JUICE
This blended juice is for the "green juice" novice.
1 organic cucumber
1 organic pear
3 large leaves organic romaine
1 large slice organic lemon
1 11.2-ounce can organic coconut water
Handful of ice

## ZESTY GREEN JUICE
I recommended using a juicer for this one.
1 organic baby cucumber
½ organic apple

Tops of organic romaine hearts, 3 bunches
½ organic lemon
2 organic carrots
Hearty handful organic kale

## And for the Last Course . . .

If I am hankering for something sweet, I prefer a yummy piece of dark chocolate and lemon and honey tea. However, the following delicious and nutritious dish finds its way to the table when the kids are looking for dessert. It provides sweetness with abundant antioxidants.

**BLUEBERRY COBBLER**
1 16-ounce bag organic frozen wild blueberries
2 tablespoons organic raw honey
2 cups granola (our favorite is a chocolate-chunk granola)

Heat the oven to 350 degrees. Place the blueberries in a baking dish. Mix 1 tablespoon of the honey with the blueberries until evenly distributed. Distribute the granola on top. Drizzle with the remaining 1 tablespoon of honey. Heat until the cobbler is bubbling and golden brown on top, approximately 30 minutes.

# Endnotes

## A Note from the Author

1. "Feng Shui," *Wikipedia*, accessed January 6, 2014, http://en.wikipedia.org/wiki/Feng_shui.

## Chapter One

1. "Habit," *Merriam-Webster*, accessed January 6, 2014, http://www.merriam-webster.com/dictionary/habit.

2. Julia Layton, "Is It True That If You Do Anything for Three Weeks It Will Become a Habit?" *How Stuff Works*, accessed January 6, 2014, http://science.howstuffworks.com/life /form-a-habit.htm.

3. "Habit," *Merriam-Webster*, accessed January 6, 2014, http://www.merriam-webster.com/dictionary/habit.

4. Dennis Price, "Retail Sales Strategies: Manipulation or Magic?" *Dynamic Business*, May 27, 2009, www.dynamic business.com.au/retail/retail-sales-strategies-manipulation -or-magic3653.html.

5. Ibid.

6. "Satisfaction with Life Index," *Wikipedia*, accessed January 6, 2014, http://en.wikipedia.org/wiki/Satisfaction_with_Life_Index. "Ethics of Altruism," *The Dalai Lama Foundation*, accessed January 6, 2014, http://learning.dalai lamafoundation.org/101/ethics1.htm. Sergei Vasilenkov, "Citizens of Poorest Countries Are Happiest in the World," *PRAVDA.Ru*, February 1, 2013, http://english.pravda.ru/society/stories/02-01-2013/123363-poor_happy-0/.

## Chapter Two

1. "About the NTP," *National Toxicology Program, Department of Health and Human Services*, accessed January 6, 2014, http://ntp.niehs.nih.gov/?objectid=7201637B-BDB7-CEBA-F57E39896A08F1BB.

2. "Why TSCA Is Flawed," *Safer Chemicals, Healthy Families*, accessed January 6, 2014, http://www.saferchemicals.org/resources/tsca.html.

3. "Questions about Your Community: Indoor Air," *United States Environmental Protection Agency*, accessed January 6, 2014, http://www.epa.gov/region1/communities/indoor air.html.

4. "Babies Born Prepolluted," *Natural Resources Defense Council*, December 29, 2011, http://www.nrdc.org/living/pregnancy/cancer-panel-warning-babies-born-pre-polluted.asp.

5. Annie Leonard, "Makeup Products: Toxins In, Toxins Out," *YouTube*, May 2, 2013, http://www.youtube.com/watch?v=9JMArdaUaCk.

6. Marian Keeler and Bill Burke, *Fundamentals of Integrated Design for Sustainable Building* (Hoboken: John Wiley & Sons, Inc., 2009), 50.

7. Walter J. Crinnion, "Environmental Medicine: Excerpts from Articles on Current Toxicity, Solvents, Pesticides and Heavy Metals," *Townsend Letter for Doctors & Patients*, http://www.tldp.com/issue/210/environmen.htm.

8. "Questions about Your Community: Indoor Air," *United States Environmental Protection Agency*, accessed January 6, 2014, http://www.epa.gov/region1/communities/indoor air.html.

9. "Post-Consumer Paint Management," *American Coatings Association*, accessed January 6, 2014, http://www.paint .org/find-your-issue/post-consumer-paint-management .html. Katherine Brown (faux painter) in discussion with the author, March 2012.

10. "Organic Solvents," *Breast Cancer Fund*, accessed January 6, 2014, http://www.breastcancerfund.org/clear-science /radiation-chemicals-and-breast-cancer/organic-solvents .html.

11. "Medical Surveillance: Formaldehyde," *Occupational Safety & Health Administration, United States Department of Labor*, accessed January 6, 2014, https://www.osha.gov/pls/osha web/owadisp.show_document?p_table=standards&p_id =10078.

12. Tracy Lydiatt, *Your Green Family Blueprint: How to Jump Start Greening Your Family—Your Way* (Vervante Publishing, 2010), 114.

13. Rachel Shaffer, "The Chemicals Called PFCs Are Everywhere, and That's a Problem," *Environmental Defense Fund*, April 30, 2013, http://www.edf.org/ blog/2013/04/30/chemicals-called-pfcs-are-every where-and-thats-problem.

14. Myron Wentz, Dave Wentz, and Donna K. Wallace, *The Healthy Home: Simple Truths to Protect Your Family from Hidden Household Dangers* (New York: Vanguard Press, 2011), 26.

15. Ibid.

16. Ibid., 28.

17. Nicole N. Soukaseum, "California State Science Fair 2006 Project Summary: Determining the Toxicity Level of Perfumes and Colognes," *University of Southern California*, http://www.usc.edu/CSSF/History/2006/Projects/J1431 .pdf.

## Chapter Three

1. Denise Reynolds, "Does Your Favorite Food Contain One of These Toxic Ingredients?" *EmaxHealth*, March 20, 2013, http://www.emaxhealth.com/1506/does-your-favorite-food-contain-one-these-toxic-ingredients.

2. "Preventing and Surviving Cancer," *NEWSTART*, accessed January 6, 2014, http://newstart.com/about-the-program/conditions/type-3-cancer/.

3. "What Is the Environment?" *National Cancer Institute*, accessed January 6, 2014, http://www.cancer.gov/cancertopics/understandingcancer/environment/page2.

4. "Cancer and Toxic Chemicals," *Physicians for Social Responsibility*, accessed January 6, 2014, http://www.psr.org/environment-and-health/confronting-toxics/cancer-and-toxic-chemicals.html.

5. Ibid.

6. Ibid.

7. "Adult Obesity Facts," *Centers for Disease Control and Prevention*, August 16, 2013, http://www.cdc.gov/obesity/data/adult.html.

8. "Data Fact Sheet: Asthma Statistics," *National Heart, Lung, and Blood Institute, National Institutes of Health*, January 1999, http://www.nhlbi.nih.gov/health/prof/lung/asthma/asthstat.pdf.

9. Carin Rabin, "Asthma Rate Rises Sharply in U.S., Government Says," *The New York Times*, May 3, 2011, http://www.nytimes.com/2011/05/04/health/research/04asthma.html?_r=2&ref=health&.

10. "Food Allergies in Schools," Center for Disease Control and Prevention, October 31, 2013, http://www.cdc.gov/healthyyouth/foodallergies/.

11. "U.S. Diabetes Rate Climbs Above 11%; Could Hit 15% by 2015," *Gallup*, October 27, 2009, http://www.gallup.com/poll/123887/u.s.-diabetes-rate-climbs-above-11-could-hit-15-2015.aspx.

12. "Constipation," *American Society of Colon and Rectal Surgeons*, accessed January 6, 2014, http://www.fascrs.org /patients/conditions/constipation/.

13. Walter J. Crinnion, "Environmental Medicine: Excerpts from Articles on Current Toxicity, Solvents, Pesticides and Heavy Metals," *Townsend Letter for Doctors & Patients*, http://www.tldp.com/issue/210/environmen.htm.

14. "What Is Body Burden?" *Coming Clean*, accessed January 6, 2014, http://www.chemicalbodyburden.org/whatisbb .htm.

15. Walter J. Crinnion, "Environmental Medicine: Excerpts from Articles on Current Toxicity, Solvents, Pesticides and Heavy Metals," *Townsend Letter for Doctors & Patients*, http://www.tldp.com/issue/210/environmen.htm.

16. Ibid.

17. Carole Jacobs, Patrice Johnson, and Nicole Cormier, "The 33 Best Anti-Aging Fruits and Vegetables," *Netplaces*, accessed January 6, 2014, http://www.netplaces.com /juicing/juicing-for-anti-aging-and-longevity/the-thirty -three-best-anti-aging-fruits-and-vegetables.htm.

18. Ibid.

19. "26 Foods High in Calcium for Healthy Bones and Teeth," *Bembu*, accessed January 6, 2014, http://bembu.com /calcium-rich-foods.

20. "Nutritionist Reveals 27 SuperFoods That Will Change Your Life and Increase Your Lifespan," *IdealBite.com*, accessed January 6, 2014, http://idealbite.com/nutritionist -reveals-27-superfoods-that-will-change-your-life-increase -your-lifespan/.

21. "How Lycopene Helps Protect Against Cancer," *Physicians Committee for Responsible Medicine*, accessed January 6, 2014, http://pcrm.org/health/cancer-resources/diet-cancer /nutrition/how-lycopene-helps-protect-against-cancer.

22. "Can Tomatoes Protect Your Skin?" *BBC*, accessed January 6, 2014, http://www.bbc.co.uk/sn/humanbody/truth aboutfood/young/tomatoes.shtml.

23. Alexandria Sifferlin, "Mediterranean Diet Improves Memory, But Not in Diabetics," *TIME*, May 1, 2013, http://healthland.time.com/2013/05/01/med-diet-and -memory/. "Omega-3 Fatty Acids from Fish Oil Protect Your Heart, Brain, and Overall Health," *Smart Publications*, accessed January 6, 2014, http://www.smart-publications .com/articles/omega-3-fatty-acids-from-fish-oil-protect -your-heart-brain-and-overall.

24. Julie Wilcox, "7 Benefits of Quinoa: The Supergrain of the Future," *Forbes*, June 26, 2012, http://www.forbes.com /sites/juliewilcox/2012/06/26/7-benefits-of-quinoa-the -supergrain-of-the-future/.

25. "Lignans," *Linus Pauling Institute*, accessed January 6, 2014, http://lpi.oregonstate.edu/infocenter/phyto chemicals/lignans/.

26. Augustin Scalbert, Ian T. Johnson, and Mike Saltmarsh, "Polyphenols: Antioxidants and Beyond 1, 2, 3," *The American Journal of Clinical Nutrition*, 2005, http://ajcn .nutrition.org/content/81/1/215S.full.

27. Stephanie Lee, "Can Tea Prevent Wrinkles?" *LIVESTRONG .COM*, October 24, 2013, http://www.livestrong.com /article/501221-can-tea-prevent-wrinkles/

28. "Tea Drinkers May Have Lower Skin Cancer Risk," *Reuters*, May 4, 2007, http://www.reuters.com/article/2007/05/04 /us-tea-cancer-idUSCOL46325320070504.

29. Elizabeth Falwell, "What Are the Benefits of Egg Yolks?" *LIVESTRONG.COM*, October 21, 2013, http://www .livestrong.com/article/526471-what-are-the-benefits-of -egg-yolks/.

30. "Avocados," *The World's Healthiest Foods*, accessed January 12, 2014, http://www.whfoods.com/genpage .php?tname=foodspice&dbid=5.

31. Ibid.

32. Joseph Mercola, "The Many Health Benefits of Avocado," *Mercola.com*, January 17, 2013, http://articles.mercola .com/sites/articles/archive/2013/01/17/avocado-benefits .aspx.

33. "Avocados," *The World's Healthiest Foods*, accessed January 12, 2014, http://www.whfoods.com/genpage .php?tname=foodspice&dbid=5.

34. Joseph Mercola, "The Many Health Benefits of Avocado," *Mercola.com*, January 17, 2013, http://articles.mercola .com/sites/articles/archive/2013/01/17/avocado-benefits .aspx.

35. "Avocados," *The World's Healthiest Foods*, accessed January 12, 2014, http://www.whfoods.com/genpage .php?tname=foodspice&dbid=5.

## Chapter Four

1. Brian Stelter, "8 Hours a Day Spent on Screens, Study Finds," *The New York Times*, March 26, 2009, http://www .nytimes.com/2009/03/27/business/media/27adco.html.

2. Dan Shapley, "Kids Spend Nearly 55 Hours a Week Watching TV, Texting, Playing Video Games . . . ," *The Daily Green*, January 20, 2010, http://www.thedailygreen.com /environmental-news/latest/kids-television-47102701.

3. Sue McGreevey, "Meditation's Positive Residual Effects," *Harvard Gazette*, November 13, 2012, http://news.harvard .edu/gazette/story/2012/11/meditations-positive-residual -effects/.

4. Wendy Jill Krom, "Michael Baime on Stress Management," *Mindful*, accessed January 6, 2014, http://www.mindful .org/in-body-and-mind/mindfulness-based-stress -reduction/michael-baime-on-stress-management.

5. Ibid.

6. Cary Barbor, "The Science of Meditation," *Psychology Today*, April 10, 2013, http://www.psychologytoday.com/articles /200105/the-science-meditation.

## Chapter Five

1. "Arianna Huffington's Smith College Commencement Speech on 'Redefining Success: The Third Metric,'" *The Huffington Post*, May 19, 2013, http://www.huffington post.com/2013/05/19/arianna-huffington-smith-college -commencement-speech_n_3299888.html.

2. Robert Pagliarini, "How to Create a New Habit," *CBS*, August 8, 2012, http://www.cbsnews.com/news/how -to-create-a-new-habit/.

## Appendix A

1. "All 48 Fruits and Vegetables with Pesticide Residue Data," *Environmental Working Group*, accessed January 12, 2014, http://www.ewg.org/foodnews/list.php.

2. "Skin: The Largest Organ of the Body," *Dr. Ramsey's Center for Natural Healing*, accessed January 12, 2014, http:// www.drramsey.com/skin-the-largest-organ-of-the-body.

# Acknowledgments

Where does one begin?

Every day, I say a prayer of gratitude for the guardian angel sent to walk by my side as I meander down the path of life. For one who is often hard to keep quiet, I am at a loss for words to express the deep reservoir of thankfulness I feel for the chance to walk hand in hand with my husband, Leif. Like any guardian angel, he has a calm, quiet, and tender spirit that emanates strength, wisdom, and unconditional love. Thank you for always encouraging, motivating, and inspiring me to be the best that I can with your "Life is good" attitude. Thank you for believing in me even when I have my doubts. Thank you for giving me the fresh perspective I sometimes need in personal matters and the business advice of a seasoned sage. This book would not have been possible without your love and support. You truly are a gift from Heaven.

Thank you to my four beautiful children, Bailey, Kiley, Clare, and Brenna, who patiently stepped up and

were willing to take on the challenges that go along with a year of Mom writing. Your sweet efforts to help each other (and Dad), whether you were braiding hair, helping with homework, reading a good-night book, or racing to tidy up before I got home, were all keenly noted and appreciated. Thank you for your hugs, texts, and handmade love notes taped to the door welcoming me home. Each and every day, you bring a smile to my heart and soul. I am so thankful for each one of you and am constantly in awe of the unique, magnificent, and radiant light you shine and share with the world. Thank you for choosing me as your hockey mom.

Great Grampa, you have believed in me and supported me in everything I stepped out to do. You were the one who was always there. I am thankful for your willingness to stay back on the bunny slope with me and drink hot chocolate; for the morning sunfish sails to the town beach and back with a capsize thrown in for strength, safety, and character building; and for a gas tank that was always full. Thank you for 11 years of school that helped me see and appreciate the big, bright world. You and Gramma were the strength and foundation that allowed me to explore and fly.

Thank you, Louise Hay, for creating the platform of Hay House Publishing, which allows authors to shine their lights and share their messages with the world. These authors in the self-empowerment and metaphysical realms gave me an awareness of a world I had never known. This knowledge inspired me to hone my message and impart it to others. This beautiful cycle of inspiration is a tribute to your flowing grace and wisdom.

Thank you, Reid Tracy, for welcoming me into the Hay House family. I am eternally grateful for the door you opened and the chance you were willing to take. Thank you for believing in my message and seeing me as a mover and shaker. I am dancing for joy to have found my tribe!

Thank you, Cheryl Richardson, for giving me clarity, direction, and a keen awareness of what it means to be a mover and shaker in this world. Your insights have shown me how to orchestrate creating a message from the heart and building a platform that is eager to receive my gifts. I am awed at your ability to target, with precision, the desire of the soul and to unlock the strength of spirit.

We are all blessed to find beacons of light along our journey. For me, Nancy Curran is one of those guiding lights. Thank you, Nancy, for helping me breathe when the wind has been taken out of my sails. Thank you for helping me recalibrate and find balance in the toughest of times. Thank you for helping me be at one with my mat instead of conquering and using yoga as an extreme workout. Your wisdom, grace, and inner knowing soothe my soul.

Along the way, I have been blessed to be introduced to the right people at the right times. These individuals have opened me to expansive ideas and possibilities that I did not know existed. I want to say thank you to Mary Dennis and Marge Richards for connecting traditional design, feng shui, and green design. You both shifted my thinking so that my thoughts and beliefs could design my world. I am grateful that your teachings were the foundations of my spiritual and business journeys. I also want to say thank you to Denise Linn, who unknowingly opened my mind to the realm of metaphysical teaching with her passion and enthusiasm. I remember walking

into a New England School of Feng Shui seminar thinking it was going to be on feng shui but finding out it was on past-life regression. Talk about spirit leading the way!

With each new seminar, program, and inspiring venue I attend or visit, I am gifted with new friends who amaze and inspire me. These individuals, with their magnificent messages and special gifts, have brought richness and vibrant texture to my life. I am thankful to have scaled red rock mountains with some (and you know who you are) and for being accountability buddies with others. I am filled with gratitude for my fellow movers and shakers at the 2012 San Diego event. Your exquisite light brightens the world. My fellow mastermind group luminaries, Calli Meister, Kimberly Kingsley, and Dennis Shaver, your support, strength, and wisdom have helped move mountains. You each embody what it means to be radiating a light from a place of inner peace and profound wisdom.

I am filled with a deep appreciation for the amazing team of people who have taken my message and made magic happen. The book-writing process is similar to the world of interior design, which is built on a collaborative model. A designer is only as good as the team of people who create the finished product. This is true in the book-publishing world, as well. Kathleen McKenna, thank you for refining my book proposal with your editing skills such that it was worthy of acceptance by Hay House. Steve Melzer, you made the video process fun and created a submission that won! Brookes Nohlgren and your team at Books by Brookes, I am grateful for your fitting this project into your schedule. Your extraordinary editing skills, which include an aptitude to organize concepts into meaningful messages, meticulous care, thorough and thoughtful research, and an ability to weave words, have honed and polished this diamond in the rough. Thank you to the team at Hay House who have helped me navigate the book-writing realm and assisted me in stepping forward with a book I am excited to share with the world. Lisa Bernier's encouraging words "It's happening, all right!" kept me believing that I was really publishing a book with Hay House. Christy Salinas and her team's creative artistry conveyed the message of the Home in Harmony Lifestyle in a picture. Her patience and enthusiasm for my color-perfectionism, especially with the color blue, is treasured. Thank you to Shannon Littrell, Richelle Zizian, and Stacey Smith, who extended a warm welcome from Hay House and assisted me in traversing the publishing landscape. Thank you to all those at Hay House I have not yet met but know will play an integral part in the success of this book and the Home in Harmony Lifestyle.

A few colleagues and friends have helped me build Home in Harmony, and their belief in me has inspired me to keep moving forward. Cindy Callan, your friendship, encouragement, and creative spirit have brought a balance to my designs and invigorated me to soar. I cherish my soul sister. Megan Antlfinger, your patience, organizational skills, and computer know-how keep me on track. Thank you for believing in me and the message and for your willingness to help Home in Harmony grow. Moira Congdon, from one hockey mom to another, thank you for the perseverance needed to build and organize the inner structure of a company. Dan Gustafson, your web magic speaks for itself. Rosemary Sneeringer, I am thankful I sat next to you at lunch in L.A. Christine Nielsen, thank you for being an artist and magician with your camera.

My dear clients and seminar attendees, many of whom have become friends, thank you for welcoming me into your homes and lives. We grow together. I marvel at the insights and awakenings that happen within me as I watch you design your inspired lives. Thank you for this blessing.

Finally, thank you to all those who supported me and my family during this project. Your encouragement, enthusiasm, and regular carpools made it possible!

# About the Author

**Christa O'Leary, MA, MFT,** is an interior designer, marriage and family therapist, and green-living expert. She teaches people how to design inspired and fulfilling lives and has been featured on CBS, NBC, and Dr. Laura. As a motivational speaker and guest on radio shows and podcasts around the globe, Christa offers people concrete solutions for creating inspired, healthy, and vibrant homes that enliven, nourish, and soothe the body, mind, and spirit.

Christa has created two successful businesses within the past ten years while raising a family of four active children. Her first company, Home in Harmony Designs, is an internationally recognized design firm catering to the discerning tastes of clients around the globe. The acclaimed fabric house Kravet Fabrics has featured her designs alongside those of some of the industry's most renowned tastemakers, Calvin Klein and Candice Olson. Her designs have also been seen on national television,

in numerous national print publications, and in international design industry publications.

Christa's most recent endeavor is being founder and CEO of Home in Harmony Lifestyle. Well-ordered and environmentally conscious living spaces contribute to good health and peace of mind; in a similar way, our inner joy and authentic light positively impact our home lives, careers, and influence on the world. The Home in Harmony Lifestyle revolves around an inspired and supportive home environment, a vital and healthy body, a calm and clear mind, and a connection to your inner light. Christa's background as a therapist enables her to guide her clients toward their best lives. She has been described as having Oprah's zeal, Dr. Phil's background in psychology and family therapy, and Martha Stewart's sense of serene home design.

At Home in Harmony headquarters, Christa continuously creates needed programs that enhance well-being in the areas of home, body, mind, and spirit. Please visit www.christaoleary.com for more information.